MW00931249

Tributes to Charlene Mitchell

Organizer and Strategist
for Freedom and Justice

Published by the
Committees of Correspondence
Education Fund

Changemaker Publications

Tributes to Charlene Mitchell: Organizer and Strategist for Freedom and Justice is published by the Committees of Correspondence Education Fund, 2472 Broadway, Rm 204, New York, NY 10025

Editors: Marilyn Albert, Timothy Johnson, Anne Mitchell, Ted Reich, Harry Targ

Layout and design: Carl Davidson

ISBN# 9-781312-627697

Order online direct at:
http://www.lulu.com/spotlight/changemaker

Table of Contents

Introduction

The 60's

The 70's

Introduction

By Mark Solomon

As the clouds of World War II darkened, a young Black girl of thirteen was confronting racism in her predominantly white Chicago high school. She had already internalized a visceral hatred for Jim Crow, refusing to accept segregated seating in the local movie and segregation at a local bowling alley. At a young age, she had already displayed boundless political energy and immense talent for organizing against injustice. During the war, she embraced the "Double V" campaign to defeat fascism abroad and Jim Crow at home – forming an early consciousness of the inextricable links between antifascism and antiracism.

Charlene Mitchell was on her way to becoming part of the historic constellation of Black women who constitute an increasingly powerful, unrelenting leadership in the struggle for liberation. Fueled by the intersecting currents of race, class and gender, Black women today are in the vanguard of movements from politics to unionism, from the arts to the law, from literature to academia. It is time for Mitchell's contributions to be acknowledged for the insights they provide to understanding the art of organizing and building solid political and ideological foundations to social movements for democracy and justice.

Charlene Mitchell's activism arose from a compound of converging influences. Her father was a laborer and trade unionist with a taste for the New Deal while increasingly receptive to politics further to the left. Her mother's religious piety, however, did not account for racial oppression that increasingly claimed Mitchell's activism. A move by the family to the Cabrini housing project in near North Side Chicago exposed Mitchell at thirteen to a strong multiracial progressive community steeped in wartime antifascism yoked to antiracism. There, she shed her mother's religious dogma, joining the American Youth for Democracy (AYD), a left youth organization with a politically broad outlook largely shaped under the influence of the Communist Party.

Later, on the cusp of adulthood, Mitchell attended the Marxist Workers' School where for the first time she read the Communist Manifesto. That classic, and the school, provided historic context and political grounding for the struggles that increasingly gripped her consciousness and activism. Marxism opened Mitchell's eyes to the systemic nature of racial oppression, when she saw that racism was no drifting force floating in political space, but was capitalism's conscious weapon in class struggle against the working class and its allies.

In 1949, Mitchell joined a multiracial group of young activists to deliver food and other essentials to striking miners in Centralia, Illinois. The miners had suffered one of the worst disasters in the country's history when in March 1947 one hundred and eleven miners lost their lives in a mine explosion. A grateful multiracial strike leadership greeted the youth, voicing solidarity and pledging to carry on. For Mitchell, that was a transforming moment signifying the liberating potential of Black-white unionism. However, it soon became apparent that patterns of segregation persisted. Mitchell and her group of Black and white activists literally reached out to Black and white miners on the dance floor, pressing conversation and igniting steps towards unity.

That incident left a lasting impression on Mitchell. From that moment, she launched a lifetime effort to build multiracial unity based on the inextricable ties between Black liberation and class struggle – with the Black struggle for freedom central to the fate of the working class movement as a whole.

The next step in Mitchell's evolving consciousness was her decision to join the Communist Party. That commitment was for her sparked by the Party's working class partisanship, its determination to fight racism and its contributions to the struggle for Black liberation. Its history included membership in the fiercely anti-imperialist Third International; it mobilized the historic global campaign to free the Scottsboro Nine; it fought to save the lives of Rosa Lee Ingram and two sons from the Georgia electric chair (a campaign that claimed Mitchell's deep involvement) and fought innumerable battles for equality in the workplace and community. The Party provided organizational cohesion and political clarity rooted in a collective system of work. That impressed young Charlene Mitchell – as did the concept of centrality of the African American struggle. For her, Party membership eschewed unmoored individualism, placing the individual within the historic parameters of universal class struggle.

That mindset provides insight into why Mitchell and her then husband agreed to "go underground" in 1952 at the apex of the McCarthyite scourge. Most of the top Party leadership had been jailed while a few evaded arrest and scores of others were convicted of "conspiring to teach and advocate the overthrow" of the government.

It was reasonable to conclude that the government was determined to destroy the Communist Party. For Mitchell, if going underground was necessary to save the organization from extinction – so be it. Thus, she and her husband shed their identities, moving first to St. Louis and later to other cities, repeatedly uprooting themselves, scrambling for employment – while providing a lifeline for "fugitive" Party leader James Jackson.

By 1955, McCarthyism had ebbed. The cold war too began to weaken as the Soviet Union sought to advance "peaceful coexistence" between competing systems. After three years underground, it was time for Mitchell to return to above ground political life. Later, in 1968 she was the Party's candidate for President, the first African American woman to take on that role, energetically traveling the country, giving eloquent political voice to a radical democratic program for getting out of Vietnam, assaulting institutional racism and advancing economic justice for all working people.

Moving to Los Angeles, Mitchell was instrumental in guiding the Che-Lumumba Communist Party club, an all-Black formation of relatively young activists of color. Che-Lumumba grated against the Party's fervent opposition to all manifestations of racial separation. However, the club's formation was in response to rising tides of radical nationalism in Black communities. Che-Lumumba believed that its organized theoretical study and engagement in struggle would help to illuminate the road to multiracial working class unity.

Among Charlene Mitchell's comrades in Che-Lumumba was a young professor at UCLA who had already earned notoriety for her brilliance and her defiant public declaration of Communist Party membership. In violation of her First Amendment Rights, Angela Davis was fired from UCLA, igniting widespread protest. Facing death threats, Davis' stored firearms were taken by young Jonathan Jackson in a desperate attempt to free his older brother George who had been unjustly sentenced to a virtual lifetime in prison. A futile attempt with Davis' guns to force George Jackson's release ended in tragedy with charges of first-degree murder leveled against Davis.

After Angela Davis' flight and eventual capture, the need to defend her against charges that could bring execution became paramount. Her arrest was viewed by growing numbers as an assault on universal human rights – with the injustices already inherent in racism threatening Davis' life and all who were victims of the carceral system. Thus, the slogan for the emerging campaign was Free Angela Davis and all Political Prisoners.

An advantage in plotting Davis' defense was the existence of her political organization prepared to render full support in the fight for her freedom. Charlene Mitchell was also was an ideal choice to coordinate a mass campaign. She had an unshakeable belief in the power of mass protest; her vast experience was a priceless asset in building alliances across ideological boundaries; she was an effective practitioner of collectivity in decision-making; in her middle years, she maintained a great capacity for work, traveling the country and the world tirelessly in pursuit of freedom and justice for Angela Davis. The seemingly endless hours of phone calls, rallies, meetings, fund raising, consultations with leaders of mass organizations, coordination with defense attorneys, travel, office and staff organizing, and above all the exercise of consummate skill in forging unity of the defense – were the essential requirements for victory cultivated in large measure by Charlene Mitchell. The acquittal of Angela Davis demonstrated the power of mass protest. It also shone a spotlight on the unjust incarceration of huge numbers of men and women, especially persons of color rotting in overcrowded prisons, victims of a repressive penal system. For the scores of people who worked for the freedom of Angela Davis, the need for a militant multiracial, multicultural organization to combat all modes of repression was incontrovertible.

With Charlene Mitchell as the leading organizer, the National Alliance Against Racist and Political Repression (NAARPR) was born. Unlike most multiracial and multicultural formations, the Alliance was a constellation of organizations and individuals, differing in scope from groups that left no space for unaffiliated activists. NAARPR was broadly based across ideological lines with links to churches and other religious organizations. NAARPR was internationalist; its engagements were global, especially contributing to the mass struggle to free Nelson Mandela. NAARPR defended indigenous communities under assault by the US government. It viewed virtually all those caught in the penal system as political prisoners – whose alleged crimes were consequences of capitalist injustice. NAARPR organized vigorous defense of civil and human rights activists under attack by racist forces. Among its most prominent cases was defense of the "Wilmington Ten" and Rev. Ben Chavis.

Crisis in the Communist Party

After a near-lifetime in the Communist Party, Charlene Mitchell in 1991 left the organization. She felt that for some years the Party had been retreating from its fervent engagement in the Black freedom struggle. Party chair, Gus Hall failed to grasp the fact that the white male factory worker was no longer fully representative of the working class. Under de-industrialization, financialization and neo-liberalism, the working class was becoming increasingly service-oriented, multiracial and multicultural, with the struggles of Blacks and all oppressed nationalities more vital – and central – to Black-white working class unity.

A second cause of disaffection was an existential crisis in the world socialist movement. The collapse of the Soviet Union cried out for a probing, self-critical analysis of the historic factors that led to the dissolution of the first modern socialist state. Such an analysis was not forthcoming. A substantial Party minority demanding internal democracy and democratic decision-making had the choice of bowing to the rigidity of the old leaders or leaving the organization.

Guiding CCDS

Charlene Mitchell was prominent among those who chose to leave the Party. She subsequently joined with others on the socialist left to build a new multi-viewpoint democratic and socialist organization. She guided the Committees of Correspondence for Democracy and Socialism (CCDS) through its early years, holding fast to the principle that democracy was absolutely essential to building socialism, and a socialist left was essential to building class consciousness.

A life of full-time activism is no way to obtain financial security – to say the least. In the mid-nineties, at standard retirement age, Charlene Mitchell, recognized that she needed steady employment with requisite benefits. Not surprisingly, her organizational skills were highly sought by the labor movement with a progressive AFSCME social services local eagerly engaging her, benefiting from her insights into labor activism and social unionism in an era of globalization.

Nearly three quarters of a century of intensive work punctuated by family tragedy took its toll on Mitchell's health. Although debilitated in recent years by illness, especially strokes that made speech extremely difficult, her fighting spirit never wavered. She died in her ninety-first year, steadfast in her devotion to democracy and socialism – her immense organizational and political skills increasingly recognized and valued by a new generation of labor, antiracist and human rights activists.

The voices of gratitude and praise raised in these pages by a cross-section of activists affirm Charlene Mitchell's place among the pantheon of powerful Black women who continue to blaze a trail to liberation of oppressed nationalities and all working people. The contributors are proud to have had a role in telling her story. Their greatest reward is the readers' determination to carry on in Charlene Mitchell's irrepressible spirit, advancing her vision of a socialist future of democracy, justice and equality.

Statement of Mourning From the Committees of Correspondence for Democracy and Socialism On the Passing of Charlene Mitchell (June 7, 1930-December 14, 2022)

The Committees of Correspondence for Democracy and Socialism (CCDS) mourns the loss of its founder, leader, and primary inspiration, Charlene Mitchell. As a groundbreaking leader in the Communist Party of the United States, from the 1940s until 1991, an organizer of the campaign to free Angela Davis, and a founder of the National Alliance Against Racist and Political Repression in the 1970s, Charlene Mitchell was one of the great twentieth  century leaders in the fight against racism, in support of the working class, and a visionary strategist for the building of a Socialist movement in the United States. She was an advocate for what is called today "intersectionality," linking the struggles of class, race, and gender. Comrade Mitchell was also well-known and admired all around the world; everywhere where there existed a vibrant socialist movement and/or government. She was particularly admired for her work in solidarity with the freedom struggle in South Africa and the Cuban Revolution.

When CCDS held its founding convention in 1994, Charlene Mitchell brought together a broad movement of communists, socialists, anti-racists, feminists, and peace activists. Through CCDS she worked to create a broad progressive majority. Her work in support of keeping the socialist vision alive in the difficult period after the collapse of the Soviet Union and the rise of neoliberal policies of the United States government during both Republican and Democratic administrations was incalculable. The rise of democratic socialism today and a new militancy among youth is a continuation of the lifetime of struggle that Charlene Mitchell carried out throughout her long and productive life. The struggles that she initiated continue today. We in CCDS and the broad left have lost a great leader.

A statement issued by the National Executive Committee, Committees of Correspondence for Democracy and Socialism

A Poem for Charlene

By Lisa Brock

I tried to find a poem,
For Charlene,
To honor her in a way that spoke to how I felt.
I looked at Maya, Lucille, Toni Cade, and Nikky
and many more
Wonderful poets writing from the bellies of Black women.
And yet, nothing was specific enough, tight enough, broad enough, radical enough, sly eyed enough, precious nor politically left enough.

If I were still a professor,
I would give my students a bio of Charlene and assign them to find a poem, the right poem, the exact poem to serve as Eulogy for her. Maybe then one would be discovered.

For now, I must write my own.

An Elegy for Charlene

From the 25th floor of your Harlem Apartment
You ruled the world.
Your house was a temple, your mind a school, your noisy second bedroom a sanctuary.
The coordinates of 25F I always forgot,
Until I saw that door sticker of Nelson Mandela marking your intentions to world.

When I think of you dear Charlene,
I think of a tower
Never uprooted from the bedrock of your foundation.

Yet like a skyscraper, you would bend and sway with the gusts of
time.
Always strategic, always tactical, always mobilizing.
A radical love of our people, all people - grounded you, uplifted
you, and kept you moving.

I saw you cry,
Only. Once.
When I interviewed you about living
With no name, no comrades, and a new baby.
Underground.
A Bleak memory of sorrow, anger and hurt.
Fittingly, the fight for Civil Rights and Anti-colonialism broke that
ugly fascist back.
And Justice movements ushered you home to Harlem.

Thank you, thank you, thank you dear Charlene.
As you move to the great socialist community in the sky, the earth,
the air, the water.
I wish you a poker game, a mystery novel, and a worthy community to organize.

Part One: The 1960s

Angela Y. Davis

Having known Charlene Mitchell through political victories and defeats, through personal tragedies and triumphs, I can say with confidence that she is the person to whom I am most grateful for showing me a life path.

What I have most appreciated over these years is her amazing ability to discover ethical connections between the political and the personal, the global and the local. I don't think I have ever known someone as consistent in her values, as collective in her outlook on life, as firm in her trajectory as a freedom fighter.

Remembering Charlene

By MaryLouise Patterson

As I write this, the moon is a hard, round, cold white ball high up in the night sky. I can see it out of my apartment window; my computer faces it. It seems to me, a full moon tonight is providential. Not in any biblical sense, but it's wanting the sharing of our memories of Charlene to illuminate her beauty, her humanity, her brilliance, her courage, her steadfastness and her love and dedication to freedom with justice, to socialism in 360 degrees. And, in so doing we elevate her life for all to see, know, admire and follow in their own unique ways. She belongs in all the history books.

Now, Charlene was 100% political. She was solidly grounded in historical materialism, Marx, Lenin, Engels, and Stalin, especially on the National Question. She'd been tutored by Cyril Briggs and others. She was familiar with the writings of Henry Winston, Walter Rodney, Cedric Robinson, Ho Chi Minh, *The African Communist*, Fidel and Mao and could explain, teach, discuss and argue about them all. She was also a lover of a good story, movie or play and if it was bad, that was even better! When it first came out, years ago now, we went to see *"Love Story"* with Ryan O'Neal and Ali MacGraw. For those who don't remember or never heard of it, it was sentimental clap-trap, a contrived Hollywood story of that perfect mythical young couple who are deeply and happily in love only to suffer the tragedy of the premature death of one of them. It was a corny predictable tear-jerker, quintessential of its time. She sat in that dark theatre and shamelessly boohooed like a baby to my unexpected astonishment! Both of us started fumbling through our pockets and purses for some Kleenex for her. When the movie was over Charlene couldn't get up, so we sat there for a few minutes watching the screening room empty out. Here was Charlene, a leader of the Communist Party, showing that she was the exact opposite of the popularized stereotype of the Communist Party female apparatchik who is emotionally empty, rigid, asexual, almost robotic. She brimmed with a profound love of humanity and freedom.

Strong, fearless, warm, generous

Charlene was 5'5", but her huge personality made her seem taller than that. She had glowing dark brown skin, a short Black afro, an open face with an easy smile and a warm generous embracing laugh that made her eyes twinkle. She was charismatic so people naturally drifted towards her. She was strong, fearless, could and did take on any big brawny racist anytime or anywhere! Her core was soft chocolate from which her love of people flowed. She also liked the hokey black and white horror movies of yesteryear with Lon Chaney and Bela Lugosi and so did I. We'd watch the reruns on late night TV. We shared a few other characteristics as well: we were both "Red Diaper Babies", both Black, both women, both mothers and both members, at one time, of the US Communist Party. Of course, she shared many of these same characteristics with most of the other Black women in the Party.

I didn't know Charlene when I returned to live in the US, after being away for 8 years, but she took me in. She had recently moved to New York City, she had an extra bedroom but most importantly she was close to my parents politically and personally. I lived with her for almost 2 years, which was convenient as she lived a mere 12 blocks north of Harlem Hospital where I started working. She wouldn't take rent from me, so I bought all or most of the food we ate. At that time I wasn't much of a meat eater, not out of any "Save the Animals or Planet" passion but because during the previous 8 years I hadn't had much of it. I thought I was doing so good, with the shopping and all until one night as Charlene opened the refrigerator door to find something to cook for dinner and not finding anything she wanted, although the fridge was full, she said out loud to me, "MaryLou (I'm MaryLouise now) "why don't you buy some meat, I'm tired of all this fish and vegetables!" Or something to that effect! I responded, "but Charlene I thought you liked what I've been buying" but she wasn't having it, laughingly saying, "I do, but go buy some meat"! And so I did.

The story I really want to share about her is the following. We were on the island of St. Croix one summer in the early 1970s. It was during the time when a number of whites, most of whom were only coming to buy up the land and businesses, were being shot and killed. It was a dark starless night and we were returning from someplace. I was driving. We were on a back wooded road and needed gas. Luckily, without knowing it, we were driving towards a gas station which lit up a crossroads ahead. We pulled into the station and up to a pump. The surrounding blackness with the glaring overhead lights made it seem like a spaceship. The station booth was some yards ahead and to the side from the pumps, in semi-darkness. After a few moments, the booth door opened and out stepped a white man, of middle age, holding, with both hands, a huge semi-automatic across the middle of his bulging gut. He stopped some distance in front of us and yelled out "what do you want"! I yelled out of my window, "GAS"! Meanwhile, Charlene had rolled down her window and began to verbally challenge the man, saying " what do you think you're doing with that gun?" "Put that down!" and so on in that vein. She was totally outraged. She wasn't having it and he got her message!

He reluctantly put the gun down and pumped our gas. When he had finally turned the gas cap for the last time, I stepped on the gas pedal so hard, pebbles flew off the back wheels – well that might be a slight exaggeration but we hightailed it outta there and back to where we were staying. I was still shaking after we got in the house, visualizing how he could so easily have shot us and probably would have gotten away with it had he done so.

The 1968 Campaign

Charlene on the other hand seemed unfazed. Perhaps she wasn't but she looked as cool as a cucumber which had a welcomed calming effect on me.

Charlene was fierce, principled, intolerant of racists and racism, sure of herself and our cause, but without arrogance. She had traveled widely: to many international liberation and Left-Communist conferences, rallies and other types of gatherings and met with world leaders and heroic activists. During her life she'd given many speeches to audiences from tens to thousands, but she was always a woman of, for and with the people, and everyone felt it. She drank Jack Daniels, played a mean game of poker, smoked Benson and Hedges and cooked better than most highfalutin chefs. She loved to have people over, socializing so easily and genuinely. And we all loved being around her. She made you feel at home, if she felt your sincerity, your honesty but especially if you were a fellow comrade in-arms or were or brought a child. She loved children and they returned that love.

Indominable spirit

So much of that was taken away from her after her stroke. But Charlene's indomitable spirit won out. Despite the fact she was left unable to speak, she made herself known to the staff of the facility where she was, garnering their respect and finally their love. The first day her hospice caregiver came, I asked her if she knew who Charlene was, she answered, "oh, the aide and I changed her just a short while ago and she told me all about her," smiling.

Charlene mentored many including me, although me - not long enough. We had our differences, as we all do, but our love, respect and trust in one another was profound and real, overriding and everlasting.

Thank you, dear Charlene, for being my sister, comrade and friend

A Committed and determined fighter

Mike Zagarell, Charlene's 1968 Running Mate for US President and Vice President of the United States

By Mike Zagarell

It was with deep sadness that I learned of the passing of Charlene Mitchell. Charlene was one of the most committed and determined fighters for humanity that I have known. Her long years of struggle for a better world showed through in all aspects of her being. She was kind, supportive, committed to struggle and uncompromising to oppression in so many of its forms. Her campaign for U.S. President on the Communist Party line, as well as her work in fighting for the freedom of Angela Davis were heroic and set an important new bar in the struggle for progress. It was truly a privilege to know her and to have been her running mate in the 1968 elections. Her contributions deserve to be long remembered by those fighting for progress today.

Celebrating Charlene Mitchell

By JJ Johnson

I met Charlene Mitchell on Nov. 5, 1968, barely two weeks after my release from the Leavenworth, Kansas military prison. The event was the New York City victory party for the first African American woman to run for the U.S. presidency.

I was enthralled. I was a political novice struggling to get my bearings, having been thrust into an environment that was foreign to the Catholic school kid from East Harlem whose political activity began with his refusal to serve in Vietnam. That night I met several friends and comrades who would have a profound influence on my political life, none more so than Charlene.

Within the next year, I was able to spend more time with Charlene. My future in-laws and wife, William Patterson and Louise Thompson-Patterson and MaryLouise, lived in an apartment on the 24th floor of one of Harlem's Esplanade Gardens co-op buildings and Charlene's apartment was on the 25th.

My discussions with Pat, Louise, MaryLouise, Charlene and others in their orbit helped me to make sense of the world and the myriad left organizations dedicated to transforming it.

Our Big Sister

As she had for many others, Charlene assumed the role of a big sister. As such, she also embraced members of my family. My brother, Darwin, considered her his mentor. Charlene was loving, but also stern. She challenged me to dig deeper and reach higher. I recall a discussion I had with Charlene while I was an editor of the *Daily World*, the official publication of the Communist Party. I was critical of a decision that was reached at a meeting of the Party's political bureau. During my discussion with Charlene, it occurred to me that even in an organization dedicated to the eradication of racism and sexism, the great Charlene Mitchell was not truly equal. White heteropatriarchy was rampant throughout the left.

I took her off the pedestal my naïve mind had erected for her. Also, as she had advised me in the past, I set out to learn about leaders like Claudia Jones, one of Charlene's heroes.

Charlene's loyalty to her friends and comrades was legendary. After I married Debby D'Amico in 1996, we continued Debby's practice of hosting an open-house gathering each Christmas evening. One year a snowstorm led us to believe we would be spending the day without our usual guests . When the front door bell rang around dinner time, I was happy, but not surprised to see Charlene, Steve and Mike at the front door. Those visits continued after Charlene's stroke, even if it meant that Steve would bring a ramp with him to roll the wheelchair into the house.

I'll always fondly remember the Charlene smile that lit up the room, our discussions and debates, our poker games, movies, concerts and birthday celebrations. And I'll continue to keep in my mind and heart the lessons of an inspiring leader and organizational genius that guided my life and work for more than half a century.

In Memory of Charlene Mitchell

By Bettina Aptheker

Dearest Charlene

So, you have passed from us. May your transition have been peaceful; in your mind's eye may you have seen the brightest of all lights. May you have felt the glowing warmth of universal love. This is how I imagine it. How I wanted it to have been for you.

We met first, I think, in about 1965 or 1966. It was in New York. There was some kind of Party celebration. I was 21, you were about 35, already a seasoned Party member who I much admired, but only from a distance.

Then we were together in Helsinki in June 1969. Do you remember? Oh, my goodness, we had such a good time, and it was also a very intense time. We were part of the U.S. delegation to a conference of the Women's International Democratic Federation. You had just finished your campaign for the U.S. Presidency on which we had all worked. You wore your celebrity with ease as women from all over offered you warm hugs and flowers.

We shared a hotel room; and, we were together through those extraordinary meetings with our Vietnamese comrades who described the war to us in such detail, with such urgency and anguish. And we stayed up late talking and trying to think of new ways we could organize even more opposition to the war when we got home.

Then one night we went to dinner together, and we had a drink or two with our meal. Then one of us said that we would go back to the hotel when it got dark, and we ordered another round of drinks. But this was Helsinki in summer, and we were very far north. At some point, it occurred to us that it was not ever going to get dark! Eventually, in the wee hours of the morning, we went back to our room to get some sleep. But on this occasion, as I remember it, we became friends. We shared so many stories from our lives, including the births of our sons. We had both suffered, but I think at the time neither of us had an idea about how to heal ourselves. And then we guffawed, and got serious, and then laughed some more, and saw in each other a gentle and loving friendship that endured.

Organizing Angela's Defense

Then about a year and half later Angela was arrested. That was in October 1970. I don't know where you were then—I think maybe in Los Angeles. But we met next in San Francisco when we founded the National United Committee to Free Angela Davis (and all political prisoners, as she insisted it be called). You became our Executive Director – thank goodness! You were a consummate organizer; in fact, you were the best organizer I have ever known. You were brilliant in knowing who to call, how to raise money, how to strategize the campaign for bail, how to reach out and build a truly multi-racial, international united front for her freedom. You saw to the building of a movement of millions across the globe. Watching you through those months I learned so much. How resolute you were, how focused, how patient, and how principled, and how you navigated all kinds of treacherous storms in our political debates around honoring the Soledad Brothers, and Ruchell Magee, and analyzing the injustice of the prison system, while holding firm to Angela's innocence. You were our political bedrock, dearest Charlene, just as Angela's mother, Mrs. Sallye B. Davis was our emotional bedrock.

June 4, 1972 – the day of Angela's acquittal – was your day of triumph, although you shied away from all the photo-taking. This was so typical of your self-effacing nature.

These are my strongest memories of our times together. Of course, we saw each other in the succeeding years, for example, at the founding of the National Alliance Against Racist and Political Repression, and at Party meetings in New York. I think at times it was hard for you to affirm some of the Party's political positions. Then in 1991 you joined with Angela and many others to form The Committees of Correspondence for Peace, Democracy and Socialism.

You struggled with ill health for many years; the stroke you suffered in 2007 was devastating. Yet, you persevered and while never regaining mobility or speech you remained fully present. In 2008 I attended a conference in New York. It was called "Black Women & the Black Radical Tradition." How you embodied both! It was held at the CUNY Graduate Center. I am sure you remember the conference and Angela's keynote. I saw you in your wheelchair before the start of the plenary session, and went over to you. I said hello, do you remember? And you beamed at me with a radiant, beautiful smile that lit up your eyes and lit up my heart. You were not able to speak. So, I stood next to you for a while leaning forward so that we faced each other and we held hands. Which was all that we needed to do.

When Kendra died in that terrible fire in June 1993 you did most of what needed to be done to organize her memorial at the church in Oakland. Your countenance that day was masked with grief. At the memorial I read a poem that contained these words. Which I offer to you now:

"Old stone, hold my soul
When I am not in this place
face the sunrise for me.
Grow warm slowly,
When I am not alive any more
face the sunrise for me.
Grow warm slowly,
This is my hand on you, warm.
This is my breath on you, warm.
This is my heart in you, warm.
This is my soul in you, warm."

All my love, Bettina.
The poem above was written by Ursula Le Guin. It appears in (her novel, *Always Coming Home*, published in 1990. The poem is called "To Gahheya")

Memories of Charlene

By Ted Pearson
December 25, 2022

Kathy and I were among a few young comrades from the U. S. to participate in a three month-long International Party School in Toronto the winter of 1966. This was where we first met Charlene Mitchell. Our routine was breakfast followed by a lecture and study, then lunch and discussion. Charlene was one of the sharpest minds in the class, unafraid to pose questions and answers as we sought to understand the basic works of Marx, Engels and Lenin. Charlene would always struggle toward the essence of what they were saying, placing them in a contemporary context. I remember especially the discussions of the national question and the liberation struggles of Black Americans in the U. S. and the French-speaking Québécois. I also remember that Charlene held her own at Saturday night poker, when Canadian Comrades Tommy Morris and Phyllis Clarke would often walk away with much of the $25.00 weekly stipend we received.

Busted by the Mounties

Our lectures included several weeks spent with Hyman Lumer on Marxist political economy. About midway through the school we were interrupted by a visit from the Royal Canadian Mounted Police (not on horses and in red coats). The U. S. comrades were told to leave the country or be forcibly deported. So we left, and continued our school in New York, where, among others, we heard lectures on Party history by Will Weinstone and Black Liberation history by Claude Lightfoot.

I later got to know Charlene better when she was Executive Director of the National Alliance Against Racist and Political Repression. Coming from the victorious campaign to free Angela Davis, which she led, Charlene was unrelenting in her determination to organize masses of people for the defense of the Wilmington Ten, Joan Little, Tchula MS Mayor Eddie Carthan, and so many more. When once I expressed sympathy with the frustration of many young leftists and ultra-leftists at the "conservatism" of the CP, Charlene said, "our work is not to lead people in frustration, but to help lead people out of it." This thought has stayed with me.

In 1981 Charlene led the CPUSA delegation to the 12th Congress of the Bulgarian Communist Party, and I was her co-delegate. This was the party of Georgi Dimitrov, who pioneered the strategy and tactics of the United Front Against Fascism in the international Communist movement in 1935, and this tradition and history was one of the themes of the Congress. Solidarity messages by leaders of parties from all over the world were delivered to the Congress, including from the CPUSA by Charlene Mitchell, a message we worked on together. To me many of the messages of other parties sounded the same, but Charlene was able to pick up on many of the subtle differences that reflected the outlook of the various parties, especially on the struggle against war and U.S. imperialism, which at that time was launching a drive to bankrupt and crush the socialist countries through the most aggressive buildup of nuclear missile capability and "Star Wars" technology. During the Congress Charlene and I had memorable meetings with Shaffiq Handal, General Secretary of the CP of El Salvador, and Volodymyr Shcherbytsky, First Secretary of the Ukrainian CP, representing the CPSU. Shcherbytsky made it clear to Charlene and me that the CPSU did not share the view of some of the other parties, that U. S. imperialism under Reagan was "insane." "They know exactly what they are doing," he said (paraphrasing). "They are trying to bankrupt us through an arms race that is unsustainable. But they will not succeed."

The Bulgarian CP Congress opened a day or two after the attempted assassination of President Reagan by John Hinckley, Jr. Comrades from all over the world were button-holing Charlene and me asking for our estimate of what it all meant. Although we knew little more than what had been reported in the U. S. and international news media, we talked, and were able to say that people should not expect any major policy shifts in the U. S. because of the assassination attempt, which appeared to be by a person acting alone.

In later years Charlene was known to me as the rock that anchored the Committees of Correspondence for Democracy and Socialism to policies of class struggle recognizing the central role in it of the African American freedom struggle, and democratic liberation struggles of other oppressed nationalities in the United States. She fought for international solidarity with liberation movements around the world.

In her last years, wracked by the effects of a stroke, Charlene always remained alert and interested in the news of the movements. She showed special interest in the struggles and victories of the Chicago Alliance Against Racist and Political Repression and its leadership in the fight for community control of the police.

Charlene Mitchell: the memory of your strength and determination and your ideas and contributions to the movement for socialism will be long remembered and should serve to inspire generations of revolutionaries in the decades to come.

Charlene Mitchell – A Remembrance

By Jay Schaffner
January 27, 2023

Charlene Mitchell was a force in my life for more than fifty years. I first met Charlene when I was 16. I had just made my first trip away from my home in Illinois – I had gone to a socialist training school of the W.E.B. Du Bois Clubs which was held at the World Fellowship Camp in Conway, New Hampshire –a big trip for a teenager from Chicago. On the way back, I attended the Special Convention of the Communist Party as a guest. This is where Charlene was nominated as the Presidential candidate, along with Mike Zagarell for Vice-President.

I remember the speech which Charlene gave. It was exciting, engaging; it was unlike many of the other speeches that I had heard while I was at the convention. Later that summer I would get to meet Charlene when she came to Chicago to meet with supporters to explain her campaign and to raise funds.

I remember a small meeting. it was just Charlene, Lou Diskin, then the education director of the Illinois Party, Claude Lightfoot, the Illinois Party Chairman, Ted Pearson, the Chicago *Daily World* reporter, a couple of other young comrades, and myself. What an honor. Claude introduced me as a "leader" of both SDS and the Du Bois Clubs. Charlene asked, but isn't he also still a high school student? Lou then interjected that it was the role of young communists to "be the best" at whatever they were doing, so as to not give the authorities any weapons to use against them. Charlene then went on to further elaborate on that. Boy, would I hear that over and over, over the years.

Here I was, a new member of the Communist Party, 16 years old, meeting with the presidential candidate, talking with the presidential candidate, and she was interested in who I was, what I was doing. And to my surprise, she even knew who my parents were.

Fast forward – two years – in February 1970 the Young Workers Liberation League was formed at a convention in Chicago. Coming together were members of the Du Bois Clubs, socialists and Marxists from Black student organizations and independent socialist youth organizations. Prior to the convention, in October, we held a teach-in on the Circle campus of the University of Illinois calling for an end to the harassment, led by Ronald Reagan, of Angela Davis who was being denied tenure by the University of California because of her membership in the Communist Party.

Later that summer Angela would be framed for the shoot-out at the Marin County, California Courthouse, and an international freedom movement would be organized, led by Charlene Mitchell.

In Chicago, the Party immediately swung into action, led by Ishmael Flory. A Freedom for Angela Committee was formed, initially led by two comrades, one African-American, one white, Sylvia Woods and Ben Green. Charlene would repeatedly come into Chicago to meet with us.

Charlene, along with Party chairman Henry Winston, helped convince us that while we were for the freedom for our comrade Angela Davis, we needed to build the broadest and widest movement that could actually win her freedom, even including people that were not necessarily convinced of her innocence. Angela was being held in solitary confinement at the time. We needed to get her out, and get bail for Angela. We shifted tactics and strategy. The focus of the movement became winning bail for Angela. Charlene made repeated trips to Chicago. She met with old friends and acquaintances from years ago when she was a teenager in the

Labor Youth League in Chicago. Many of them were now leaders in trade unions, in the Democratic Party, in church and civic organizations. She helped convince them that bail for Angela was a just and righteous issue – the right thing to come out for. If they could do what they are doing to Angela today, what would stop them from not going after others, like yourselves tomorrow. She won them and others over. She helped convince others – both liberals and the left.

Leadership in the Free Angela committees

Charlene also fought to change the character of the Chicago Committee for the Freedom of Angela Davis and All Political Prisoners. Something new was happening – Black women were coming forward demanding freedom for Angela Davis, and these women wanted and needed to be in the leadership of the Chicago committee. They flocked to Sylvia and to Charlene, and the Chicago committee changed. Charlene made numerous trips to Chicago to meet with the Chicago committee, and while in the city would meet with the leadership of the Party. I was part of the Chicago Party leadership from 1969 – 1974, until I moved to New York City, and was often part of these meetings with Charlene.

I remember meeting with white trade unionists with Charlene, and hearing her work to convince them that the fight for Angela's bail was a trade union issue, a democratic issue. It helped convince me. I was working in a small machine shop, composed of Polish, Ukrainian, other white, African American and Hispanic workers. I started wearing a Free Angela button at work. Soon I was able to convince the majority of workers to also wear an Angela button, partially because it was getting under the foreman's skin.

On June 4, 1972, Angela was acquitted! Sylvia Woods said we are going to hold a celebration, and I helped get the biggest venue in Chicago – McCormick Place. Three weeks later we held a massive rally. Similar victory rallies, organized under the leadership of Charlene and Louise Patterson, and the leadership of the Communist Party, were held in other major cities across the country.

The following year, Charlene, working with others, pushed and pulled to form a united defense organization – what would become the National Alliance Against Racist and Political Repression. It not only included what were the Committees to Free Angela Davis and All Political Prisoners, but also the movement to defend Puerto Rican political prisoners and the Puerto Rican Socialist Party, the defenders at Wounded Knee and the American Indian Movement, the defenders of Chicano land and Chicano studies, the early victims of the attacks on Blacks studies, and the defenders of women's right to choose and abortion rights and gay rights. Charlene helped forge a big tent that brought all the victims together, that truly "an injury to one, is an injury to all."

More Victories

Soon the National Alliance would bring the Defense of Joann Little to national prominence and win her acquittal, along with that of the Rev. Ben Chavis and the Wilmington Ten. It was Charlene and the Alliance that brought national attention to the fight against the death penalty and that North Carolina at that time had the largest number of prisoners on death row, and the largest number of African Americans on death row, and then the most Jim-Crowed and gerrymandered voting districts in the country.

Over the next decade I would see Charlene at meetings. We worked in different political areas, we were friendly, but not really friends.

That changed around 1985. I was then the president of Anniversary Tours, a travel agency that specialized in travel to the Soviet Union, Eastern Europe and Cuba, specifically in group tours, and which pioneered "people-to-people" tourism. Charlene began to work part-time at Anniversary as a bookkeeper. We began to socialize more, and celebrate holidays together. Charlene also had a pretty good idea of what my thinking and attitudes were as to what was happening in the socialist countries, as I was making regular trips to the Soviet Union and other countries to plan future travel programs for Anniversary. Charlene also saw that I was essentially withdrawing from actively participating in the current work of the Party, even though I was still a member of the Central Committee, and still attended national meetings, but now largely did not speak.

In April 1988 Carl Bloice, who was the resident Moscow correspondent for the *People's Daily World*, was making a return visit to the United States to report on developments in the Soviet Union. Charlene was going to host a breakfast for Carl at her apartment, and invited me. She told me that there would be other members of the Central Committee there to hear what Carl had to say. Since there was going to be a report by Carl later that week, it was obvious to me that this was an opportunity for members of the Central Committee to get together, who were not necessarily "happy" with the direction of the Party leadership. Charlene asked me to think about it, and that if I decided to attend or not attend, to just leave it at that and say nothing. I agreed, and decided to attend. That Sunday, I went to Charlene's and boy was I surprised at who was there. Pleasantly surprised!

Unpredented: A Minority Report

And that started the closest relationship that I had with Charlene. Later that summer, as an outgrowth of that April, we kept meeting, and we asked additional members of the Central (National) Committee to meet with us. That summer we decided that we would do something unprecedented, or unprecedented in most of our memory – after the main report at the August National Committee meeting we were going to ask to give a Minority Report. Twelve members of the National Committee asked for a vote to give a report to be presented by Comrade Charlene Mitchell outlining differences of opinion and views within the leadership that were not being shared with the full membership of the National Committee. All hell broke loose. After the meeting was recessed and heads and noses were counted, democracy prevailed and the report which we had already distributed was voted on to be read and discussed by the meeting. Later we would debate and vote that it also be shared with the full membership.

For the next two years we worked closely, working to unite as many as possible, to win people to see that a new way of thinking was possible. Charlene had to continuously work to convince comrades like myself, who did not think that the Party could be changed; that we needed to work to win as many comrades as possible to see that a change was possible, that the obstacle to change was Gus Hall and company. In the end we won between one-third and one-half of the Party membership to a new way of thinking, but a change in the leadership and structure of the Party was not possible. The culture and habits of the Party were too fixed, the ideology was too ingrained.

Working with Charlene, Danny Rubin, and with other comrades in districts around the country, we pushed and cajoled, getting people to talk to this one and that one, reaching out to people that we had worked with years and years ago, to reach with a simple message calling for discussion and renewal. We went over lists of names, calling people, talking, meeting people we hadn't spoken to in years, reaffirming our belief in both socialism and democratic struggle as a prerequisite for socialist democracy. And a prerequisite for both was the centrality of the struggle for equality and against racism, which we felt was slipping and had slipped in the Party.

We worked to unite the broadest number of comrades on the need for a change, but could not discuss, let alone get agreement on what type of alternative form of organization, what strategy for fundamental change and what tactics for change were needed. So we set hundreds of dedicated socialists adrift without an organizational or political home for them to go to.

The Berkeley Conference

Months later we would gather in Berkeley to form the Committees of Correspondence for Democracy and Socialism, it was a new beacon for socialists and the left, but it did not really have an agreed upon ideology or program. Over the course of the next few years I would work closely with Charlene as we struggled to build the Committees, Charlene as the National Coordinator and one of the CCDS' national co-chairs, myself as the organization's treasurer.

No matter what the politics, Charlene always had time for people, never forgetting about one's family, always remembering Judith, my parents, Judith's father and aunt, our children. The personal concern was part of her strength as an organizer and leader.

Charlene was a true force of nature, a loving, caring, comrade, a fighter for the people.

Charlene Mitchell Shaped My Future

By Randy Shannon

Charlene Mitchell had a profound and lasting impact on my political development. I want to briefly recount some key moments in the development of my political consciousness to show that Charlene's impact on me was timely and decisive.

In my freshman year at Duke I was invited to join a sophomore history seminar called: Democracy, Communism, and Fascism. It was taught by a young professor, whom I later figured out was a leftist. I chose as my class project to write a paper on the Spanish Civil War. I read a lot of books and learned about the fascists, the progressive government, the socialists, the Trotskyists, the anarchists, and the communists – all of whom had organized contingents under arms to oppose Franco. My study led me to conclude that the communists were the best led and organized political group opposing Franco.

In early 1967 Duke Administrators sensed the rising social tension and alienation of our generation of students. Their answer was a series of speakers and they campaigned to turn out the whole student body. The students usually filled the auditorium. There were many speakers, but I remember three very well: Frances Fox Piven, Dean Rusk, and Herbert Aptheker. Aptheker held a little Q&A session after the speech; it was crowded and I was there because his critique of the Vietnam War and US government policy was radical.

I had joined the Duke "Liberal Action Club" in my freshman year after two seniors visited my dorm room and invited me. I participated in several activities. It was my first organized progressive group. In the summer of 1967, we joined Vietnam Summer and polled working class neighborhoods in Durham, mostly tobacco workers. I was quite impressed by the overwhelming majority of people who were against US involvement in Vietnam. At that point I naively concluded that our government was not a democracy and should be overthrown!In the middle of my junior year, I withdrew from Duke to become a full-time organizer for the Southern Student Organizing Committee. I began working in a campaign to organize anti-war committees on every college campus in NC. Then I spent almost a year organizing students in Columbia, SC. While hanging out at a GI Coffee House in Columbia, I was approached by one of the Coffee House workers and told that a GI wanted to desert from Ft. Jackson and asked if I could help. So SSOC set up an 'underground railroad' and got this GI to Canada.

In the late Spring of 1968, I moved to Nashville and established a newspaper, *"The Phoenix"* to cover the rapidly growing student movement in the South that became close to the civil rights and the union movements. I traveled most of the South contacting activists organizing against the Vietnam War, supporting the struggle of black students for civil rights, equal funding, and anti-racist struggles, women's liberation, and the miners' Black Lung movement.

In the summer of 1968 Charlene Mitchell brought her campaign for President to Nashville. Charlene spoke to a small group, mostly SSOC members and activists. She made a lasting impression on this 22-year-old activist because her critique of US imperialism, racism, subjugation of women, and anti-unionism was thorough, reasoned, articulate, calm, and persuasive. She answered many questions, and I finally became aware that there was a real communist party in the United States that included African-American leaders.

In summer of 1969 SDS demanded that SSOC dissolve itself because it was too liberal. We gathered all the SSOC activists and organizers at a camp in Mt. Beulah, MS. SDS leaders including Mike Klonsky attended, but there were also two reds meeting with us in Mississippi, Mike Zagarell, who had run for VP with Charlene Mitchell and Michael Eisenscher. After the Mt. Beulah meeting voted to liquidate SSOC I joined at least six SSOC organizers to rebuild the Communist Party in the South. We organized clubs in Louisville, Nashville, Birmingham, Jackson, and Memphis.

In 1970 I began a working/learning relationship with Charlene as I worked in Nashville to set up a "Free Angela Davis" committee. This committee was very influential at the black colleges and in the housing projects, where the committee concentrated its work. A few years later I worked with Charlene to organize a local chapter of the National Alliance Against Racist and Political Repression.

The 'Charlene School of Organizing'

Charlene schooled me and many other activists in the South and across the country in the tactics and strategy of moving grass roots people into thinking, action, and organization. Charlene's "school of organizing" led to several important progressive alliances, and to many progressive organizers. The success of Charlene's strategy of building independent left/progressive organizations led to the growth of independent leftists. I was with Charlene and others in 1991 at the initial formation in Cleveland of what became CCDS. Although Charlene told me she didn't agree with Gramsci I felt that she was the Gramscian leader of the left in the USA.

Charlene Mitchell, Henry Winston, and Claude Lightfoot were my advisors and leaders for most of my adult life. Winnie paid close attention to our growth in the South and we studied his *"Strategy for a Black Agenda"* and followed his articles and speeches closely. Claude visited us in Nashville several times helping us analyze past successes and failures and plan the next steps to achieving our goal of building a progressive coalition in the South. Claude also told some thrilling stories about his underground life during the McCarthyite "Red Scare." I trusted these leaders because I knew they were close to Charlene.

First Memories of Charlene

By Marty Price

My first memories are when Charlene ran for President in 1968. As a Red Diaper baby, I was keenly aware of who she was, and how history was being made. In 1969, we in the Oakland Direct Action Committee, were in contact with her through Kendra Alexander as we were doing security for Angela Davis. Later in 1969 I met with Charlene in NYC as we had our first national committee meeting to build the Venceremos Brigade. I assured her there'd be no Red baiting going forward, in the Brigade movement. Returning home, I then met with Kendra, and the Che Lumumba Club which was the backbone of our Los Angeles delegation. Over

time and after the 20th Anniversary Brigade I was recruited to the Party by Pat Fry and Billy Proctor. It became an epiphany for me in my own personal development.

Memories, memories

By Tilly Teixeira

Charlene was a close comrade as well as family friend since the late 60's. Memories, memories, times at the Cape, political and social, here in Boston. Charlene was a close comrade to my husband and became part of my family over the years.

My last fond memories were from Cuba in 2007 where Charlene was in treatment and a guest for over a year at their "Instituto Neurologico " for rehabilitation after her stroke--I stayed there, as did other friends and family for a month's stint as companion and aide. Just a note about Cuba and international solidarity. The Instituto Neurologico near Havana tends not only patients from all over Cuba, but maintains part of the site to service patients from abroad –some as political guests from the worldwide movement –some as "paying guests" and some from an agreement with Mexico to treat selected patients with specialized needs.

It was a profound education. Not only did I learn about health care for stroke and physical disabilities which serves me now as a benchmark for disability care, but also gave me time to live and learn with ordinary Cubans in everyday life. As one of the other "patients in my small casa", a Catholic priest from Mexico stated that he had the choice of a facility in the US or there in Cuba. He said "in the States I might get 1 or may be 2 hours of therapy a week, but here you know the routine".

The routine was 2 1/2 hours of physical therapy twice a day, morning and afternoon week days and 2 ½ hours on Saturday. As needed and with Charlene, one of those sessions was speech therapy.

A Compliment Long Remembered

By Carl Davidson

I first met Charlene Mitchell at the National Conference on New Politics, held in the Palmer House in Chicago in 1967. As the gathering proceeded, a 'Black Caucus' had formed, and it had put forward a 13-point platform, along with a demand for greater representation in the leadership going forward. As the debate progressed, the percentage changed from 25% to 50%--I could be wrong, my memory is not all that reliable, and the accounts I could find online varied. Blacks made up about 15% of the delegates and represented nearly all trends in the Black movement.

As this issue was coming to a head, several non-Black speakers had opposed the proposal as undemocratic, representing neither the majority of the delegates nor a majority in the country.

As a National Secretary of SDS at the time, I was pissed and got called on stage, and was handed the mike. "The basic mistake here is not seeing this as a political question, It's not a mathematical question or one of statistical measure. What this proposal is affirming is that the key to victory in any U.S. movement, or in the revolution overall, is a strategic point, that the core alliance in our struggle is the general movements of workers and students on one hand, and the African American peoples struggle on the other.' I said a few things more, but I also used an old trick I learned from Carl Oglesby. 'Eat the mike, get close and speak loud.. everyone will stop and pay attention.' It worked.

As I was getting off the stage, an attractive and older (by my standards at the time) African American woman came up to me. 'I'm Charlene Mitchell from the Communist Party, and I want you to know you just made one of the more revolutionary speeches at this entire event.' I thanked her, and even though I wasn't enamored of all the CP's views at the time, I was a friend of Jack Spiegel in Chicago, and knew there were many good people in it I liked.

Later that day I spotted her near the stage, frustrated and arguing with TV news people about how their overuse of glaring lights was being disruptive. I went up, and asked her what was wrong. 'No problem,' I said. I searched around for their power cords, found the key link, yanked it from its socket, then its extension, then tossed the cord in some obscure garbage can. Years later, she didn't remember much of my speech, but was still vividly impressed with my 'solution' to her problem.

Charlene Mitchell: Honoring a Committed life

The following statement was issued by the Communist Party USA on Dec. 27, 2022, on the occasion of the passing of Charlene Mitchell.

From the Peoples World

The Communist Party USA pauses for a moment to dip its banner to honor the life of Comrade Charlene Mitchell, who died recently at 92. Mitchell was a lifelong activist and joined the Communist Party at 16. She soon became a leading figure in her local Los Angeles Che Lumumba club in the 1960s and in the CPUSA nationally.

In 1968 Mitchell made history as the CP's presidential standard-bearer, becoming the first African American woman to run for the

Oval Office, along with youth leader Mike Zagarell as vice president.

When Angela Davis was framed and charged with murder in California, Mitchell, along with Henry Winston and others, became a chief organizer of her historic defense, securing first bail and later acquittal after a long ordeal.

Charlene then helped found and lead the National Alliance Against Racism and Political Repression (NAARPR), a national organization committed to upholding the rights of victims of state repression. The Alliance successfully pursued the cases of Joanne Little, charged with kidnapping a prison guard and Rev. Ben Chavis and the Wilmington 10 falsely accused of arson in North Carolina.
Mitchell served on the National Committee and National Board of the Communist Party for many years but left the party during the political storms of the early 1990s citing ideological differences. Soon after, she became a founder and leader of the Committees of Correspondence for Democracy and Socialism. In later years, the party and Comrade Mitchell put aside past differences and worked closely together on a number of projects, including the founding of the Black Radical Congress and fighting the right-wing danger.

After suffering a debilitating stroke, Mitchell remained active for many years, a tribute to her fighting spirit. We extend our deep revolutionary condolences to Charlene Mitchell's family, comrades, and friends as we honor a life well-lived.

Part Two: The 1970s

Charlene Mitchell – Our Movement Mother

By Mildred Williamson
Januuary 7, 2023

In the early 1960s, I was a preteen, and deeply moved by the nightly television news reports with film coverage of the Civil Rights Movement, especially the young people whom I could see fighting off police with their dogs, high power water hoses, yet singing freedom songs before and after the brutal treatment, even while jailed. They were fearless! I wondered, how could I find a way to be a part of this? I didn't see that type of activity in Chicago where I grew up, but later as a teenager, I found myself present when Dr. King came to Chicago. I was fortunate to hear him speak at my church.

I soon joined other students to establish a new Black Student Association at my high school. This was hardly comparable to the heroic struggles I saw on television, but it was a start. We even had some great teachers who supported us and sponsored our Black Student Association and our demand to have *Before the Mayflower* by Lerone Bennett Jr. as required reading for our US History class. We actually won that struggle! Baby steps indeed...

Assassination of Fred Hampton

Little did I know what was yet to come. In my senior year of high school Fred Hampton, chair of the Illinois chapter of the Black Panther Party, was murdered by police along with Mark Clark on Chicago's West Side. That same month, I met Willie J Williamson, the person who later would become my husband and remains the love of my life. However, at the time he was in the military in another state, and I was still striving to finish high school at home.

And then – I learned about the Angela Davis case and attended a local rally and concert for her freedom, where my favorite saxophone artist, Gene Ammons performed in solidarity for her release. Of course, it was electrifying!

I was getting closer, but not quite there in my quest to meet and learn from seasoned activists in this all-important Movement. I saw speeches from afar, such as Rev. Jesse Jackson in the early days of Operation Breadbasket (now Rainbow PUSH Coalition). I heard Dick Gregory and Dr. King, but no one whom I could easily spend quality time with to learn more.

So of course, life happens. I finished high school, got a part time job, and started attending classes at Malcolm X College in Chicago, along with Willie, because by then his military service was completed. He was living in Chicago, and we decided to get married. We were both committed to being a part of this Movement!

Well, through friends who worked in the same factory as Willie, we met other friends who were activists, and they told us about a conference that was taking place in Chicago in support of African Liberation, and help was needed to organize it. That 1973 conference actually was the founding of the National Anti-Imperialist Movement in Solidarity with African Liberation (NAIMSAL), with Oliver Tambo, Henry Winston and Angela Davis as keynote speakers. That was a significant turning point in both of our lives. We enthusiastically got involved and met so many people locally and nationally, who would become lifelong friends, and importantly, mentors and comrades.

Meeting Charlene and her team

We hit the jackpot of our lives that year when we met Charlene Mitchell, Franklin Alexander, Kendra Alexander, Victoria Missick, Anne Mitchell, Ishmael Flory, Sylvia Woods and so many others. These folks took us under their wings and showed us how to organize, strategize and mobilize people for justice and freedom. We learned about international struggles, colonialism, Marxism, the Labor Movement and the meaning of solidarity. We learned a class analysis of racism and powerful strategies to fight against it. We learned about race/class/gender intersectionality before the concept was popularized.

Charlene was a master organizer, strategist, teacher and mentor. She taught us the art of persuasion and showed us how to connect the dots to see how one social justice struggle relates to another – locally, nationally and globally. She taught us how to figure out the key tactics of building coalitions, all while standing on solid principles. She could bring all kinds of people together for all kinds of social justice struggles. She was a master analyst of political situations and freely shared her wisdom. She taught us everything with patience, love and grace.

The impact of Charlene on me was so profound, as it built my confidence beyond anything I had ever imagined. It turns out that the skills of political analysis and principled Movement building are absolutely applicable in all life endeavors. Everything from navigating the everyday racism and sexism of school and work situations, child rearing, community struggles and even issues of self-care and well-being, I could reach back to lessons learned and recall gems from Charlene that served as guidance and a way forward.

What a special person to have had in one's life! I want all who read this to know that Black women Mothers of this Movement are the anchors – and Charlene Mitchell was like no other. Love you Charlene, forever will!

Among the First to Lead This Struggle: The Legacy of Charlene Mitchell

By Frank Edgar Chapman, Jr.
Dec 28, 2022

Frank E. Chapman, Jr. is currently the Executive Director of the National Alliance Against Racist and Political Repression. From 1961 to 1976 he served a prison sentence for a crime he was falsely accused of, until he won parole due to a campaign led by Charlene Mitchell, Esther Cooper Jackson, Angela Davis, Hershel Walker and others. He was granted clemency by the Missouri Governor in 1981.

The 1970s: Frank Chapman, Charlene Mitchell & Hershel Walker.

I want all the revolutionaries and young freedom fighters who are members of the National Alliance Against Racist & Political Repression to join us as we dip our banners of struggle for our dear comrade, Charlene Alexander Mitchell, who was born June 8, 1930, and died on December 14th.

In the last week or so, I've read thousands of words on Charlene's passing and her becoming part of the pantheon of revolutionaries who have gone before her.

A lot of things have been said about her particular political contributions: her rise to leadership in the Communist Party; her being the first Black woman to run for president; and the tremendous contributions she made in defense of democracy and the freeing of hundreds of political prisoners during the 1970s and 80s. But I'm afraid that what has been written so far, as deserving and fitting as it is, misses one very critical point about Charlene's life and her legacy. I would say she was first among those in the 20th century - along with Angela Davis, Henry Winston and William Patterson - Black Communists – that created one of the most powerful and inspiring movements in the Campaign to Free Angela Davis and All Political Prisoners.

It is amazing to think of what that movement accomplished: in over 60 different countries and over a thousand cities in the United States, the call went out to free all political prisoners at the time. The call included those who had gone to jail for political reasons, but also those who had gone to jail for other reasons – in the main, being trapped in ghettos and the constant cycles of crime - but who later on became political prisoners by their fight for their rights as human beings while they were in prison, like the Attica brothers and George Jackson. Like myself.

I was languishing in a dungeon called the Missouri State Pen and fighting an uphill battle to overturn a sentence of life plus 50 years when the National Alliance was founded by Charlene, Angela, Anne Braden, and 700 other brave souls in Chicago in 1973. In 1976, I came home from prison because of the Alliance, and in 1981 I was granted an executive clemency by the governor of Missouri because of the unspeakable power of the movement led by Charlene Mitchell. Charlene organized and fought not only for Angela Davis, but she also helped to free many more from the hellholes of America's prisons.

A deeper meaning

Because of the accomplishments of the movement she led, I believe Charlene's legacy has a far deeper meaning for Black liberation than what is expressed in anything I've read thus far.

This is the legacy that I want to bring attention to. This is the legacy which I think has fueled more than anything else the fires that we still see burning in the struggle for Black liberation to date. This fueled the fires of the George Floyd and Brionna Taylor rebellion. The fact that the Alliance was engaged in this rebellion in a leadership role is no small tribute to Charlene's historic leadership in the founding of this organization almost 50 years ago. The Chicago Alliance winning the enactment of the ordinance Empowering Communities for Public Safety is a tribute to her, as well.

That's the legacy that she left us. She left us a legacy of struggle. She used to say, "Organization plus unity plus struggle equals victory." We still have that in our literature. And every time we put that in our literature, we honor Charlene Mitchell because she's the one that gave us that.

She said, "Lead our people not in their frustration, but lead them out of it." Every time we organize the fight to free a political prisoner; every time we organize a fight against police crimes and police brutality and murder; every time we work with families who have lost loved ones; with families who still have loved ones that are languishing in prison; every time we do this here and now, we pay tribute to Charlene Mitchell, who started this fight for us almost five decades ago.

Charlene was the architect and the strategic leader of the most massive defense campaign in history - defending the Black liberation movement, the democratic rights of workers and oppressed people, and the rights of revolutionaries, be they communists, the nationally oppressed, or both.

We in the National Alliance Against Racist and Political Repression dip our banners of struggle saluting Charlene Alexander Mitchell while we proudly continue as the torch carriers of her living legacy.

Tribute to Freedom Fighter Charlene Mitchell

Dr. Benjamin F. Chavis, Jr. is President and CEO of the National Newspaper Publishers Association (NNPA) and Executive Producer/Host of The Chavis Chronicles on PBS TV stations throughout the United States

By Dr. Benjamin F. Chavis Jr.
National Newspaper Publishers Association President and CEO
December 21, 2022

All people throughout the world ultimately benefit from the singular and collective sacrifices of a few monumental and courageous freedom fighters who have dared to speak out, stand up, and act valiantly on behalf of the universal cause of freedom, justice and equality. In the course of human history, I have been privileged personally over the past 75 years to meet and to work with some of those global "freedom fighters."

Charlene Alexander Mitchell (1930-2022) was an admired courageous international freedom fighter. On behalf of the Wilmington Ten and all political prisoners in America, we humbly and solemnly pause to render a memorial tribute to our beloved Sister Queen Mother Freedom Fighter, Charlene A. Mitchell.

From being born in Cincinnati, Ohio on June 8, 1930, to moving to Chicago where at the young activist age of 16, Charlene joined the CPUSA, and then she went on to reside in the heart of Harlem, New York where for over 60 years she effectively led hundreds of grassroots, national, and international campaigns for freedom and equal justice.

Charlene Mitchell passed away on December 14, 2022, in New York. I know that her legacy and ideals, however, will live on for many future generations to come.

Who was the key organizer and strategist of the successful global campaign to free Angela Davis from political prosecution and imprisonment? It was Charlene Mitchell. Who was the visionary activist organizer of the National Alliance Against Racist and Political Repression (NAARPR)? It was Charlene Mitchell.

In addition to the support and leadership of the United Church of Christ Commission for Racial Justice and the Wilmington Ten Defense Committee, it was in fact the gallant leadership and global mobilization efforts of Charlene Mitchell, Angela Davis and many others in the NAARPR that helped to free the Wilmington Ten, Charlotte Three, Joann Little, and so many other political prisoners throughout the United States in the 1970s and 1980s.

James Baldwin's Praise for Charlene

In the early 1980s during a video filmed dialogue between James Baldwin and me at Dooky Chase restaurant in New Orleans that focused on Black American oppression and liberation, I recalled that Baldwin affirmatively asserted that, "There is no question in my mind that Charlene Mitchell remains the Joan of Arc of Harlem because she dares to utter unspeakable truth to power."

But I also witnessed the personal side that intersected with the extraordinary ideological and organizing genius that Charlene

Mitchell embodied 24/7. She was a devoted and caring mother to her son, Steven Mitchell, who also became a labor organizer and representative.

My mother, Mrs. Elisabeth R. Chavis, and the mother of Angela Davis, Mrs. Sallye B. Davis, and Charlene Mitchell would find quality time together, even while traveling from city to city to free other political prisoners, to talk about the importance of family in our long-protracted struggle for freedom in America and throughout the world.

I will always remember the loving smile on Charlene's face and that unforgettable twinkle of solidarity in her eyes whenever she discussed and planned how to organize and to win victories over peoples' oppression.

How should we say thank you adequately to leaders and freedom fighters who have passed away? We all should keep fighting for freedom and hold dear to the passion and principles that they lived by and represented. Long live the spirit, love, memory and legacy of Charlene Alexander Mitchell. Rest in Power and in Peace (R.I.P). God bless.

Charlene Mitchell, Always a Friend

By Coraminita Mahr
Vice-President, 1199SEIU, Retired

Charlene Mitchell was one who you could always depend on to be there if you needed a friend.

When I moved to New York with my husband and daughter, I had the opportunity to witness firsthand the depth of Charlene's heart, compassion, and concern for the vast number of friends, comrades, and "extended family." Charlene took us into her home when our housing commitment fell through.

She was there for so many - as a leader, as a teacher, as a role model, and confidant. Her home was the venue for social gatherings and dinners, poker parties, and meetings. I think "hostess with the mostest" was coined for Charlene.

She had the energy, patience, and willingness to be a mentor for whoever needed her guidance, advice and counsel .

Over the 50 years of knowing Charlene, I never witnessed or experienced a change in how she valued and cared for her friends and family. She was steadfast in her faith to her extended "family."

In spite of the multitude of tasks and responsibilities she took on throughout her years in the struggle - she was present. I admired her for her discipline, her work ethic, her commitment to fight and struggle for the rights of working people, the imprisoned, freedom fighters. She taught me the true meaning of what it takes to be committed to struggle and win.

My memories take me to the work of one of the most important organizations and movements I've ever been a part of - the National Alliance Against Racist and Political Repression. Her leadership combined with her ability to bring and inspire other brilliant legal minds, organizers, elected officials and strategists to join this movement was the recipe for the successful outcomes and release of so many political prisoners, civil and human rights activists wrongfully accused and imprisoned- Angela Davis, the Wilmington 10, Johnny Imani Harris, Joanne Little, Mayor Eddie Carthage (to name a few) including the fight to end police brutality and crimes which continues across the country .

Tens of thousands were masterfully mobilized nationally and internationally under its banner through marches, political campaigns, and mass education.

Victories too numerous to list. I can only say, Charlene's ability to galvanize the masses, and teach others the importance of developing, identifying and utilizing the right tools, with the right combination of expertise, strategy and tactics was a masterful art. Her ability to allow others to take credit and shine was a masterful art as well. Today, The Chicago Alliance Against Racist & Political Repression continues to win victories with learned lessons from Charlene around police brutality and police crimes .

The organizing carried out under Charlene's leadership were the richest, most rewarding experiences I ever witnessed.

I'm proud to have been a member of Charlene Mitchell's family and will cherish her memory forever.

Tribute to Charlene Mitchell

By Maria Ramos

Hearing that streets in New York City were made of gold, my parents migrated from Puerto Rico in the late 1940s. Instead of finding gold, they joined the ranks of the unemployed, poverty and lived in welfare tenement buildings in Chelsea, a Manhattan neighborhood. I was brought to 235 West 23rd Street, which was family court at the time. Of course I did not realize that many years later I would be sitting in that same building with Charlene Mitchell and Angela Davis, as a member of the Communist Party USA.

I was asked to join the Free Angela Davis Committee when a fellow student and City College of New York saw me collecting signatures on Angela's petition. I made new friends in the Young Workers Liberation League, a youth organization with CPUSA. We had a community center in Harlem at 145th Street and that is where I met Charlene's son Steve Mitchell. Steve changed my life. He asked me to come to his home not too far from the community center to meet his mom Charlene and Angela Davis herself. I was humbled and honored. I was subsequently asked to do personal security for Angela. If she was willing to risk three life sentences, then sure why could not I give up one life for hers. Through this work I became close to Steve and his mom. Steve, Ron Tyson, Kevin Tyson, Charlene's nephew Aaron, and I became a close knit security team. We would meet, strategize, and have fun together. We all would hang out at Charlene's.

Charlene became very special to me, not only politically but personally. She would always cook dinner for us and I had a seat at her dinner table. I enjoyed many Thanksgiving dinners with them and, yes, she was an excellent cook. She also helped me navigate through some of my relationships, both good and bad. I remember she once said, knowing that I was heading for a very bad break up with someone whose name I shall not mention here. She said "I hope you are prepared." A warning about my impending heart break.

Our 'Harriet Tubman'

I had the opportunity and the honor to introduce Charlene Mitchell to an audience. I introduced her as "Our Harriet Tubman of Today." Being on security, I always had the opportunity to watch this amazing woman give leadership to the National Alliance Against Racist and Political Repression. She was brilliant in strategizing. Whether it was on how to free the next political prisoner, or how to get Congress to extend and enforce the Voting Rights Act in 1982. She gave leadership in helping to free Mayor Eddie Carthan, the first Black Mayor elected in Mississippi since Reconstruction in 1877. Charlene changed my life in so many ways. Charlene was my leader, my mentor, and, in many ways, my caregiver. She even became Godmother to my eldest daughter Naima Ramos Chapman.

I will always love Charlene for believing in me, trusting me with her life, and showing an entire generation that "we can fight back and win."

Tribute To Charlene Mitchell

Born in Cape Town, South Africa, Trevor Fowler was a political exile in the United States, Canada, and Botswana. Following the 1994 democratic breakthrough in South Africa, he served in several responsible positions in Government. Currently he serves as a Commissioner of the Financial and Fiscal Commission of South Africa and is Adjunct Professor at the University of the Witwatersrand School of Government.

Charlene Mitchell with Nelson Mandela and Angela Davis

By Trevor Fowler
January 2023

I met Charlene, as the keynote speaker, at an event on March 8, 1971, International Women's Day, as part of the campaign to Free Angela Davis. Charlene was the national coordinator of the National United Committee to Free Angela Davis (NUCFAD). The event at Gordon Bell High School auditorium in Winnipeg, Manitoba, was organised by the Communist Party of Canada. I was asked to be the programme director for the event.

A powerful speaker

The acquaintance with Charlene, made on that day, was the start of a friendship with an extraordinary woman who contributed to my life in a way which is immeasurable – as she did with many people like myself. I had never organised national or international campaigns nor was I a public speaker when I met Charlene. In fact, when I was to speak at the International Women's Day event to which Charlene was invited, I froze for what seemed an eternity. It is through the coaching of Charlene and the National Organiser of NUCFAD, Shyrlee Williams, that I overcame the fear of public speaking.

Charlene had this incredible ability to communicate the complex mechanisms of building organisations and campaigns into simple learnings. Charlene's achievements and contribution to building socialism came not only from her activities within the Communist Party (CPUSA) but from activities with mass organisations and campaigns. The understanding of mass work was the basis of the success of the campaign to Free Angela Davis and many others through the National Alliance against Racist and Political Repression (NAARPR).

Charlene's success in organisation stems from the ability to communicate with ordinary people. When Charlene spoke publicly, it was not simply to tell the story of the campaign but how to take the message to other people. The very essence of Charlene's public speaking was to proselytise. Charlene had the ability to interact with all kinds of people be they young or old, rich or poor, working class or not, religious or not.

Freedom for Ben Chavis

Charlene was fearless in confronting injustice. She initiated the organisation of a rally in Raleigh, North Carolina to highlight the killing of a young Black man in Greensborough as well as for the release of the Wilmington Ten who were wrongfully convicted in 1971. The rally mobilised 10,000 people in a very conservative state. Again, this successful campaign resulted in the release of Rev. Ben Chavis. Furthermore, the case of Chavis versus the State of North Carolina was a major victory because the convictions against the Wilmington Ten (10) were overturned by the Federal Appeals Court which found that the prosecutor and the trial judge had violated the Ten's constitutional rights. The Ten were pardoned by the Governor of North Carolina in 2012.

On one occasion, Charlene drove me to the airport after I stopped in New York on a flight from Canada. I discovered that en route to Canada the airline agent removed the wrong ticket, namely the return ticket to South Africa. I tried to explain the missing ticket to the agent, to no avail. At that point, Charlene intervened, got the attention of the agent who conceded the error and allowed me to board the flight.

Understanding and building organisations was really Charlene's forte. In 1977 there was a World Conference against Apartheid and in Solidarity with the Peoples of Southern Africa. An important event was a press briefing by Joshua Nkomo and Robert Mugabe who announced the formation of the Patriotic Front between Zimbabwe African People's Union (ZAPU) and the Zimbabwe African National Union (ZANU). Behind the scenes, Charlene met with Oliver Tambo and requested the campaign to release Nelson Mandela be changed to Free Nelson and Winnie Mandela, because a campaign for the freedom of a husband and wife would have more public appeal. Indeed, the campaign resulted in Nelson and Winnie Mandela being household names throughout the world.

The support of Charlene, the NAARPR and actress Frances Williams, who was chair of the National Anti-Imperialist Movement in Solidarity with African Liberation (NAIMSAL) led to the formation of broad-based campaigns in Los Angeles in 1980 which garnered the support of Los Angeles Councilman Robert Farrell, Assemblywoman (later Congresswoman) Maxine Waters and many others. These efforts ultimately led to the formation of the Free South Africa Movement spearheaded by Randall Robinson, Mary Berry, Walter Fauntroy and Eleanor Holmes Norton in Washington, DC, which was a turning point because it resulted in the Comprehensive Anti-Apartheid Act of 1986 which legislated comprehensive sanctions against Apartheid South Africa.

Charlene Mitchell lived a full life and made the world a better place! Long live the spirit of Charlene Mitchell! Long live!

Speaking Truth and Shining a Light

By Michael Honey

Emeritus Professor and former Harry Bridges Chair of Labor Studies at the University of Washington

Charlene gave us remarkable leadership in the campaign against racist and political repression, and it made all the difference. I was based in the South from 1970-76, as southern regional director of the National Committee Against Repressive Legislation, on the National Alliance Against Racist and Political Repression Board, and with the Southern Conference Educational Fund. I learned so much in that time period from her that gave me a framework for the rest of my life as an activist and movement scholar. Academia can sometimes seem trivial in comparison to the work that Charlene did. I remember inviting her to speak at the North American Labor History Conference at Wayne State University in Detroit sometime in the early 1990s, I think. She gave a marvelous talk. What really delighted me, though, was how she directly chastised participants because so few people of color were in attendance. She didn't let that slip by. Someone else might have just complained privately about it, but she let us know in no uncertain terms that what labor scholars were doing was inadequate and frankly, embarrassing to us all.

Thank you Charlene for always speaking the truth and shining a light on what we need to do to make a better world and a radical movement.

My Two Stories About Charlene

By Dr. Lisa Brock
Professor Emeritus, Kalamazoo College
June 6, 2023

Charlene Mitchell was special to me in many ways. She was a role model for how to build multi-racial, Left-centered but broad movements for human rights and justice. Just watching her work was like being in school. She knew how to see potential in young people and teach you through action.

I will share two stories. I met Charlene in 1977 when I joined the Washington DC chapter of the National Alliance Against Racist and Political Repression at age 19. I was a junior at Howard University. The NAARPR was organizing a national Free the Wilmington Ten Rally in 1978 and Charlene, Frank Chapman, and other national leadership were in town. We were meeting the day before the rally and Charlene gave me $10 and told me to go have lunch with Angela Davis. I was so surprised, and star struck, that I have no memory of talking to AYD (and I am sure she has no memory of it as well), but the gesture was a nod to my potential, and I felt more confident in my work.

Second was when the Wilmington Ten got out of jail and they were coming to All Souls Church in DC for a welcome home event. Charlene asked me to post up as security for Congressman Ron Dellums. Here I am 5'1" doing security for a well-known Congressman who was over 6 feet. It was scary and exhilarating at the same time. Charlene was a role model, a consummate organizer, a mentor, and a teacher. And she also provided housing in Harlem whenever I needed it. She leaves a huge legacy and high bar that I have tried to live up to. I always ask myself: What would Charlene do?

A Patient Mentor, a Trusted Friend, Always a Comrade

By Ronald A. Tyson
Chair, English Department
Raritan Valley Community College

I met Charlene Mitchell for the first time in the fall of 1970. I had joined the Young Workers Liberation League in late summer, and when Angela Davis was arrested in October 1970 in NYC, I began to work with other folks to secure her freedom. That is how I met Steve Mitchell, her son, and he introduced me to Charlene.

Through the years, there were the poker games at her apartment in Harlem, long political discussions into the early morning hours, plenty of good bourbon, and lots of laughs.

Charlene was a patient mentor, a trusted friend, an always-there comrade. She was a good listener, and I could tell her just about anything/everything I was experiencing, whether personal, professional, or political. She taught me how to own up to my mistakes and to always take responsibility for my actions.

I sharpened my political sensibilities under her guidance. There is a line in Chimamanda Ngozi Adichie's novel, *Americanah*, in which the narrator speaks of how her relationship with another character made her feel good about herself. Knowing and working with Charlene made me feel good about myself in many ways: I knew that I was on the right side of history, that I was doing what I needed to do for African Americans, that I was doing what I needed to do for my self-actualization. The only other thing that requires stating . . . Well done, sister. Well done!

Charlene: Seared in Our Minds and Hearts

By Kevin Tyson

I was 16 years old when I joined the Youth Committee to Free Angela Davis, encouraged by my brother to help secure freedom for one of the most phenomenal activists of our time. Shortly after, I met Charlene Mitchell as she crossed the country and traveled internationally to organize activists, actors, scholars, religious leaders and just about anyone that would listen to win Angela's freedom, occasionally stopping in our shared Harlem.

Charlene welcomed me in her house as one of her children, and I was amazed by her brilliance, charm, and delivery. But it wasn't until a year later after Angela was freed, and one of her nephews moved to New York that I would spend hours at Charlene's house and listen to her articulate the need for unity and struggle, while eating some of her home-cooked wings and greens and exposed to her motherly love and caring. This side of Charlene would have just as much of an impact on my life as her teaching me and others how to organize and strategize for liberation. Charlene was a master at the art of coalition building, and I witnessed this numerous times, including as the Alliance made house in North Carolina and worked for the freedom of Rev. Ben Chavis and Joann Little.

A Profound Effect

Charlene would talk about how all of her "children' turned out ok, but I wonder if she really knew the profound impact she had on us. Whether complimenting or chastising us, it would be done with grace and determination to ensure we understood her point. Her love for humanity was unparalleled, and her commitment to freedom was second to none. To hear Charlene talk about her ex we watched *"Boyz in the Hood"* together at the movie theatre. Her first response at the end was "talk about a message movie", and we reflected on Dough Boy's comments about how what happens periences would keep you in amazement for hours, and her analysis of events, whether internationally or down the street, would keep anyone's attention. I remember how moved she was when in the 'hood is treated as a statistic and not a human tragedy, or sometimes doesn't even make the news. Decades later, as we are witnesses to the destabilization of the Black community and we are in search of change and hope, we look towards Charlene as a model for inspiration and dedication to build a new community and a new world. Even as she later had difficulty communicating, you were clear where Charlene stood on an issue.

The footprint that Charlene has made on the world is seared in our minds and hearts. I am confident that Charlene is still organizing and strategizing, and still cooking wings and greens with the ancestors.

Tribute to Charlene Mitchell

Adjoa A. Aiyetoro is a lawyer specializing in representing the imprisoned and in reparations for Africans and African Descendants. She has worked in the US Justice Department, the American Civil Liberties Union, as well as the National Conference of Black Lawyers.

By Adjoa A. Aiyetoro

Charlene Mitchell exemplified a leader for radical change who knew the importance of and practiced the art of organizing broad networks working to end racist repression and to build a just world. The slogan she penned for the National Alliance Against Racist and Political Repression (NAARPR) - "Organization plus unity plus struggle equals victory"- is a formula for success of campaigns for justice.

I met Charlene Mitchell in 1979 after I joined the DC Branch of the National Alliance Against Racist and Political Repression. When I first met Charlene, I experienced a woman who was warm, direct, knowledgeable, incisive and welcoming. As I worked with the Alliance over many years, she challenged and encouraged me to do more and be more.

Charlene broadened my worldview. I saw more clearly how government authors attacks on Black people to keep them in a subordinate position. I saw that these attacks, most frequently through the criminal legal system, are unleashed either because of direct challenges to racism by political activists or, because of the need to repress Black people in general. Charlene taught me, through her imprint on the Alliance, the importance of organized, collective struggle against repression. She had a significant effect on the trajectory of my career, most particularly, on the lens through which I view addressing matters of racial, economic and social justice. Charlene was an example of a strong, brilliant Black woman leader, committed to ending government-supported and-led repression of people of color. Ashé, Charlene, Ashé.

For Charlene

Sandy Frankel was a staff member of the National Committee to Free Angela Davis and both Sandy and Kay Anderson were staff members of the National Alliance Against Racist and Political Repression, under Charlene Mitchell's leadership.

By Kay Anderson & Sandy Frankel

How to say Goodbye...

To a mentor whose patience was only rivaled by her fierce commitment to justice;

To a leader who truly engaged and enjoyed every single person in her life;

To a woman whose pleasure in competition matched her embrace of beauty;

To a leader who found more capabilities in her staff than we knew or ever imagined we might have;

To an organizer who brought together with the most committed, fascinating, and joyful people in our country to struggle for freedom;

To a sensitive woman who welcomed us and our families into hers;

To a friend who never, ever ceased to be supportive and caring when tragedy snaked into life;

To a woman who enriched our lives with memories that sustain us always.

Charlene, there is no way to say goodbye ~ we'll simply continue to carry you always in our hearts.

Dreams of a Different World

By Mary E. Charlson

Charlene was dedicated to confronting injustice everywhere. When Charlene arrived, she always held the room. With a quiet and unrelenting intensity, she focused on the issue at hand, and there always was a pressing issue. The fight for the freedom of Angela Davis was spearheaded by Charlene, who gave it all her energy and skill.

Her leadership brought together people from many perspectives and places and created a new organization to fight against racist and political repression. Many battles for justice followed as well as new initiatives to fight police crime, for freedom for Nelson Mandela and South Africa. Through it all, Charlene maintained her commitment and persevered through the most difficult of times.

She had dreams of a different society and world, where there was truly justice and freedom for all. She spent her life fighting to achieve those dreams, pulling together as many like-minded people as possible. We all hope those dreams will be realized. She has many friends and admirers for her unwavering courage and dedication.

But most important to her was her family, especially Steve, who has stayed with Charlene all the years, as an active member of the civil rights movement, but also as a dedicated loving son.

Charlene's Special Place

Jack Kurzweil is a San Francisco Bay Area activist, and was active in the campaign to free Angela Davis.

By Jack Kurzweil

Charlene was the only person in my life who could phone me, tell me what to do, and have me do it right away.

Tribute to Charlene Mitchell

By Dessima Williams

Charlene Mitchell was someone I admired from afar and then I got to know her and admired her even more. I would see her at conferences, busily directing others and putting things in place as well; I would admire her as she chaired meetings and delivered statements and I would think ---what a deep and thoughtful woman leader, what a powerful person presenting herself so simply with grace and zero pomp! Most of all, I would learn from Charlene, that one can be effective without jumps and shouts but with a solid message that connects to those listening.

I was blessed to be a guest in her home and to be at the receiving end of her hospitality and her learnedness as she toured me through the rich contours of how she went about organizing. Charlene introduced me to some of the most dynamic Caribbean Labor Movement leaders in New York. I believe it was Charlene or Margaret Burnham or Angela Davis who included me in the mailing list of the Committee of Correspondence which I loved because I love receiving letters, and the Corresponder was fresh and relevant news and analysis in the post - like a personal letter from several friends.

Charlene was one of a network of wonderful US political organizers whom I was privileged to work with —Jack O'Dell, Josephine Butler, Acie Byrd, Carlottia Scott, Mr. Murphey from Baltimore, Jim Drew, Lennox Hines, Wilhelm Joseph, Deborah Jackson, Maurice Jackson, Johnetta Cole, Barbara Lee, people of knowledge, integrity and commitment to justice. All of you and thousands more were committed to the Grenada Revolution. Forty-four years later, I say thank you to Charlene and thanks to all of you.

Dear Charlene, thank you for your life and service and may your soul rest in perfect peace and your legacy live in the continuing service of others.

Dessima Williams is President of the Grenada Senate

Charlene was my true mentor

By Judith L. Bourne, Esq.

A Buddha is a person who is awakened, or enlightened, to the true reality of life. A fundamental principle of that reality is that all persons, simply by virtue of their humanity, are equal and are entitled to respect.   A person whose life exemplifies this principle is akin to a Buddha. Throughout her life, Charlene Mitchell satisfied this criteria.

Anyone familiar with US-based left activism over the past 70 years knows of Charlene Mitchell the committed revolutionary, the astute organizer, the woman whose speech could inspire and energize a crowd and whose clear and focused analysis illuminated the path that was needed to move the struggle forward.

I met Charlene shortly after I completed law school, just after the successful campaign to free Angela Davis, and in the context of the anti-apartheid movement. Her commitment, her knowledge and her wisdom immediately attracted me, but I was somewhat in awe. The warmth with which she embraced me and my commitment soon put me at ease and ready to learn the many things that she taught, largely by example.

All of the tributes honoring her inspiring leadership are appropriate and well-deserved, but I wish most to honor what I see as the source, the bedrock, of that enormously creative and effective force - her deeply embedded and indomitable humanism.

Charlene never saw "the masses"; she saw people whose lives, hopes, dignity and agency were being crushed by exploitation, and she joined with them, and rallied others, to engage in the multi-faceted struggle to end that exploitation, no matter what the immediate cause.

But her humanism was not only manifested in her lifelong struggle for a world of peace, justice and equality. It was evident in the way in which she effortlessly acknowledged the inherent dignity of every human being with whom she had contact. If course, like everyone, she had her quirks and she certainly wasn't easy. But her criticism was never personal, and it was never nasty. She had a clear-eyed wisdom that was focused on the goal and the purpose, whether communal or individual.

Charlene became the big sister that I didn't have. She held the secrets that I didn't want known but that I had to tell to someone, and I knew that my confidences would never be betrayed. She would offer advice on such matters only when asked or when it would have been disloyal not to give it.

Charlene was a true mentor, she showed how to uphold the ideals and principles that she espoused by living them, and she sought to help everyone that she worked with to develop both their leadership and their supportive abilities, without being didactic.

I am proud and thankful to have been a recipient of her mentorship, and to have been her friend and comrade.

Part Three: The 1980s

Auntie Charlene Mitchell

Giulio Sorro teaches high school in San Francisco, California. He was taught under the wings of Charlene, to continue the legacy of freedom fighters.

By Giulio Sorro

Your large Cheek bones
You said were like those of the people of South Africa
Where Nelson Mandela greeted you with tea in the morning
When you stayed at his home

I meet your shoulder at the same time I meet you
There I slept on it as you sat between me and Jordan
In the back seat of the Blue Corsica
On the way to Tahoe
Kendra in the front
Franklin driving
How did we fit all our stuff in that car?

You taught me ways to deal with racism
When on that trip Kendra flashed on the young white girls
Who told us,
Who told you
Told the Black people
"I'm glad you did the dishes"
I looked in the mirror and asked
"Who am I?"

Me and Jordan had to sleep somewhere else when that guy
With the other guys slept in his room
Chris Hani was shortly killed after
And every time Angela would come stay with you at 25F on 147th
I would sleep on the couch
The same one we used to sit and talk and drink cheap white wine
called Woodridge that I would go buy at the liquor store on Lenox
There I learned
You were an audio book and all I had to do was listen and keep
asking questions.

"The FBI 1600 pages on me kept great notes of our meetings"
Charlene if you were to go back what would be something you
would have done different,
"!1968 was such a powerful time and when I ran we could have
done something big, something more, looking back now"

Beyond the politics was the fried fish you made as we sat together
looking over Manhattan 25 floors up
Was the room you opened up to me when I moved to New York
Was the home that was always there
I still got my keys

On that building on 147th
"they knew I wasn't a Christian on Sunday but when they raised
the rent everyone would start knocking on my door"
The same door Uncle Steve would come through and say "Momma"

The First horse I rode on was your father's
Black Communist Marxist Revolutionaries
Henry Winston Presente!
Paul Robeson Presente!
In All God's Danger Presente!

Kendra and Franklin Alexander Presente!
Uncle Carl Bloice Presente!
The last time I read your name was in the preface of Assatas's book,
And how about your book, we gotta ask Gina
Auntie Charlene Mitchell,
Presente!!!

Charlene Mitchell

Pat Fry is a journalist and was an early staff member of the Committees of Correspondence for Democracy and Socialism.

By Pat Fry
January 2, 2023

The progressive movement has been standing tall on the shoulders of a giant and master of movement strategy and tactics for racial equality and working class unity - Charlene Mitchell – presente: 1930 – 2022. We will miss our leading voice for peace and the working class.

Charlene was a mentor to many of us who learned what it meant to be a strategist and internationalist. Charlene represented the Committees of Correspondence for Democracy and Socialism at the 100th anniversary celebration of the Communist Manifesto in Paris. She foretold the growing proletarianization of the US working class, particularly of physicians and social workers. Charlene often said "we don't discuss strategy and tactics enough." Charlene was part of the US delegation to observe the first free democratic election in South Africa defeating apartheid. Nelson Mandela won his freedom after a worldwide campaign against apartheid.

Charlene emphasized that strategy and tactics were essential in identifying the key social forces necessary upon which to build the foundation of a broad popular democratic coalition and movement, starting with the interconnectedness of the key forces of women, and the oppressed peoples of the multi-racial working class. She taught us that the key to building unity and the anti-racist struggle movement was building the trade unions – the key training ground. She would always say "if class is not in it – we can't win it."

Charlene put those skills to work in the successful fight to rid the island of Vieques of US military occupation and bombardment. Charlene organized her fellow social worker trade unionists to travel to Vieques to protest the US military presence joining the local community activists there. Upon leaving the island Charlene insisted that we stop at the local hotel casino and play a game of craps. She was an excellent strategist at poker as well.

Message for Charlene

By Roger Green
Former member NY State Assembly

Our human family has from time to time been uplifted by the work of some extraordinary public servants for justice who have sacrificed their lives in the struggle to defeat political oppression, economic exploitation, and cultural degradation.

This most certainly is the legacy of our beloved sister in struggle, Charlene Mitchell. In Charlene we witnessed a unique leader and organizer possessed with a radical imagination, who understood that a member of a vanguard was not on top, but always on tap.

Humility with integrity

Charlene's sacrifices were legendary because they always seemed to balance humility with an unbending integrity. In fact, these were the qualities that she bequeathed to a long list of union leaders, anti - racist activists, peace activists, women rights activists, and elected officials, whom she bequeathed with her enlightened advice and counsel.

In deep respect for Charlene's legacy of work and her inspirational spirit we are moved to say, "Rest in peace and power, our beloved Charlene".

Charlene Guided Me with Discipline and Love

By Rafael Pizarro

I loved Charlene so much. What I remember is a woman who corrected my mistakes before I made them. She demanded a kind of discipline in both theory and action. I also loved how the Cubans respected her. I remember when I traveled with her for a conference of the Latin American Left with Lula, Ortega, and others. We were treated like diplomats.

A remembrance? Walking off the plane in Havana and being greeted by the heads of the Party and whisked off to eat cuchifritos and drink mojitos while they checked our luggage.

Hay Amor, Charlene

Esperanza Martell has worked since the 1960s for the independence of Puerto Rico, where she was born, to end the US military occupation of Puerto Rico, and to free Puerto Rican political prisoners. She is an educator, writer, artist, and mother. She lives in New York City.

By Esperanza Martell

Remembering Sister Charlene Mitchell for her support in the Campaign to Free Puerto Rican Political Prisoners. Rest in Power. Hay Amor, love

Everyone Knew Charlene

By Ira Grupper

Charlene had invited me to accompany her to a conference in Athens, Greece. Can't recall the year...Everyone, it seems, knew her—from all over the world.

A Socialist and Feminist

By Mark Mishler

Legendary organizer and radical socialist feminist thinker and activist Charlene Mitchell has passed at the age of 92.

I was one of thousands of fortunate people who were lucky to have the opportunity to know, learn from, and work with Charlene in her long activist life.

I missed her path-breaking 1968 campaign for President as the candidate of the Communist Party (buttons above), but had the opportunity to work with Charlene, among other things, in the National Alliance Against Racist & Political Repression, on her 1988 campaign for U.S. Senator from New York (see the still completely relevant *"Do you have to be rich to live in New York?"* flyer (above), and in the work that resulted in the creation of the Committees of Correspondence in the early 1990s. I arranged for Charlene to speak in Albany on police brutality in 1991 (see "*How Many Videotapes Will it Take*"

Charlene may be best known for leading the successful, against enormous odds, international campaign to free Angela Davis in the early 1970s. Charlene was a great leader, a brilliant strategist, and a warm, caring person. She will be sorely missed.

Part Four: The 1990s

Condolences: South African Communist Party

By Chris Matlhako
Former SACP Secretary for International Affairs

On behalf of the communists and progressives in South Africa, the South African Communist Party extends and expresses its profound condolences to the family and friends of Charlene Mitchell – a staunch fighter for justice, nonracialism, and an internationalist. Comrade Mitchell carried the common struggles of the downtrodden of the world and illuminated these to many who crossed her life. We've indeed lost a true internationalist fighter. However, we are comforted in the knowledge that her life was not in vain. As we say in the global South – A Luta Continua! Venceremos!

Memories of Charlene

By Mark Solomon

A few years ago, at a testimonial for Charlene, her then employer, trade union leader Charles Ensley, said with perceptible tongue-in-cheek that she was "bossy." I was chairing that event – responding that if Charlene was "bossy," the progressive movement urgently needed more "bossy" people like her. In today's parlance, I probably would have said that she exuded "good bossy" in the spirit of John Lewis' "good trouble."

Actually, Charlene was a practitioner of democracy manifested in a fervent dedication, with appropriate acknowledgement of the contributions of individuals, to the primacy of the collective. In the formation and activation of the collective Charlene located the key to building a majority capable of winning victories and setting mass movements on the road to transforming change. With that vision, she hammered at the centrality of Black liberation inseparably connected to the struggles of the working class. Embedded within her insistence on collective engagement was a profound grasp of the interpenetration of race, class and gender – well before  "intersectionality" became widely recognized on the left. With an understanding of how to build alliances and deepen social consciousness, Charlene advanced the concept of a Progressive Majority, which through learning, action and unity would grow in consciousness to become a dominant irreversible force for change.

Against sectarianism

That Progressive Majority, in Charlene's view, rejected sectarianism, political narrowness, humorlessness and instead, no matter how difficult the circumstances, expressed confidence in the working class and its allies, in the ultimate defeat of racism and misogyny and in a socialist future. Working with Charlene over a ten-year period as a fellow co-chair of the Committees of Correspondence for Democracy and Socialism, I cannot recall a single instance when democratic norms were violated, where political differences were personalized, or where the struggle for survival of a small organization led to declining morale.

On the contrary, Charlene's toughness and durability played a decisive role in sustaining the organization and holding fast to building a vessel of diverse political currents. At the same time, that toughness was complemented by an indivisible sense of warmth and abiding concern for the wellbeing of colleagues.

More than a half century of experience and hard work involved many tasks of varying magnitude that were pursued by Charlene with equal vigor, whether collating documents or addressing a gathering in Paris of international scholars to observe the 150th anniversary of the Communist Manifesto.

To the end, Charlene, hobbled by massive strokes most likely driven by great family tragedy, never lost her fighting spirit, her political acumen or her vision of a socialist country and world founded on the elimination of all forms of oppression.

Charlene is irreplaceable. However, we can strive to emulate as much as possible her fighting spirit, her organizational and political skills and her boundless humanity. She has entered the pantheon of great Black women and women of all races. Let us draw strength and clarity from her life and labors and follow the road to peace, democracy and socialism that she has helped illuminate for present and future generations of working people.

Charlene Fighting for the Soul of the Revolution: An Appreciation

Barry Cohen was an early staff member of the Committees of Correspondence for Democracy and Socialism

By Barry Cohen

Chronologically, Charlene was part of the Silent Generation. Boy, does that tell us how misleading it is to paint an entire age cohort with a single brush

.

Charlene's life was defined by her refusal to be silent in the face of injustice or intimidated by repression. She refused to accept limits on imagining a world without exploitation and oppression. She already believed as a teenager that another world is possible and throughout her long life she devoted all her energies to organizing to achieve it. It was in this sense that Charlene always viewed herself as a revolutionary.

Charlene came of age in a world of colonial empires, at a time of McCarthyism, Cold War, and Jim Crow. In fact, the Smith Act trials, the HUAC hearings and other anti-Communist repression did produce a lot of fearful, conformist thinking and shameful behavior. It ruptured the progressive traditions in American society. It produced what Hollywood writer Dalton Trumbo called "The Time of the Toad", when thinking was criminalized and the informer was exalted as a hero.

In that atmosphere silence and conformity was certainly the easy way, the safe way, the personally advantageous way. But the Communist Party had a proud and sometimes heroic record standing up to repression, racism and Jim Crow, and union-busting. That is the path that attracted the teenage Charlene and is the path that she chose.

It was the path of defending democracy, which came dangerously close to extinction in the McCarthy period. For her and in reality, standing up to anti-Communism was a defense of the rights of all.

Creating space for a new generation

When Charlene became the presidential candidate of the CP in 1968 she blazed a trail as the first Black woman nominated for that role. But in that role she led in other ways as well. Her candidacy challenged the anti-democratic laws that still prohibited Communists from running for public office in some states. It defied and helped to usher into oblivion the Subversive Activities Control Board. It eroded the fog of fear around the fake Communist menace. It created space for a new generation to think about electoral struggle as having revolutionary potential.

As a presidential candidate in 1968, Charlene confronted head-on the anti-Communist rationale that cloaked the conduct of a colonial war by the United States in Vietnam.

My close working relationship with Charlene began in another period, in the context of a different challenge.

It has to do, I believe it is fair to say, with how a revolutionary fights for the soul of the revolution.

Over a period of decades, a deepening crisis affected the Communist movement worldwide. The depth of the crisis wasn't clear to the people in its midst (or to those outside it either, for the most part). At issue, among other things, were the model of organization, relations with other political forces, and the viability of the Soviet system – the conception of a modern socialist society. This was, of course, a very complex process and so were the reactions to it. But to put it in capsule form, some forces in the movement responded to the crisis by seeking wide-open discussion, rethinking and reform, while others doubled down on existing formulations and practices, even reinforcing them.

This, to me, is "the soul of the revolution." A movement that seeks to change the world must constantly and intensively study reality, revising its conceptions and practices.

The gradual crisis headed toward an acute phase in the second half of the 1980s. This played out differently in different countries, but it was a global phenomenon. In the United States, the "doubling down" tendency dominated the leadership of the CPUSA.

At that time – early 1990 – I was the editor of the *People's Weekly World*. Sentiment among the leadership and staff of the paper was overwhelmingly in favor of the "open discussion" approach and this was the editorial policy we adopted. This led to increasing tensions with the Party leadership. Actually, relations broke down almost completely.

The differences became so deep and systematic that in preparation for an upcoming convention I wrote and presented to a leadership body a critique of a proposed draft main convention resolution.

A day or so later Charlene visited my office at the paper. She sat down and said "A group of us in the leadership have been meeting to discuss the direction that things have been going and what you wrote is very much in line with what we've been thinking. Would you like to join us?"

And that is how I came to join the meetings that had been going on for some time in Charlene's Harlem apartment.

The group had been meeting quietly, but its intent was to end the practice of keeping secrets in a small circle, suppressing debate and hiding differences of opinion. On behalf of the group, I drafted what we titled *A Message to the National Committee*, laying out our thinking on many aspects of the situation and our policies. The Message, signed by 13 members of the NC, was presented to an NC meeting in May 1991.

The response from "the administration" was to denounce the document as "factional" and to demand that it be withdrawn. In August the situation became even sharper, as Gus Hall – who despised glasnost and perestroika – adopted a "neither condemn nor condone" stance toward the bungled coup against Gorbachev. The NC voted by a narrow margin to reject Hall's position and to condemn the coup, which the *Peoples' Weekly World* duly reported.

The situation was clearly critical. The Message group then took a bold step. We decided to make a last ditch appeal to the membership to open up a bold discussion and to avert a split.

James Jackson and Marilyn Albert with Charlene

We formulated what we called *The Initiative of 100*, seeking the signatures of 100 respected activists in the Party. One hundred signatures, in the face of the furious response it was sure to meet, seemed like an ambitious and perhaps unachievable goal. Would there be that many who would dare to speak out knowing that they would be subjected to shunning and attacks from comrades – or former comrades? In the end, much to our surprise, 1300 – more than a third of the membership – signed the *Initiative*.

The central proposition posed in the *Initiative* is the need for democracy to be married with the ideals of liberation: "The lesson which must be taken to heart, above all, is that there is no other force than the conscious activity of working people which can effectively forge the way to a new society or guarantee its development. That is why democracy, the means of organizing that force, must be constantly strengthened in society, in working-class and people's organizations, and in the Party itself.... We need to update our concept of socialism.... Life has shown that the command-administrative economy and the fusion of state and party were obstacles to the development of a humane, democratic and modern socialism."

Not a Straight Line

This speaks again to the soul of the revolution. The Russian literary critic and democrat Nikolai Chernyshevsky once observed that "the course of history is not like the Nevsky Prospect" – a straight street through the center of St. Petersburg. To make history you have to have the courage to strike out on a new path, even when you cannot see exactly where it will lead.

Individuals matter. This is a truth I was able to observe up close in these events. There were a small number of people – you could count them on one hand – without whose actions these events would have unfolded differently. Charlene is the first among them.

And from there, things happened quickly. At the 25th Convention in Cleveland all of the "dissidents" were removed from leadership. The staff of the *Peoples Weekly World* returned to find themselves locked out (and the short factual account of the convention cut from the paper at the printing press).

In short order, the New York and Northern California districts – by far the largest – voted to disaffiliate from the CP.

We – and by now the "we" embraced an array of left forces from various traditions – then organized a conference in the Bay Area on the theme of Perspectives for Democracy and Socialism in the 90s. That conference, in turn, planned for the organization that became the Committees of Correspondence for Democracy and Socialism.

The period leading up to the 25th Convention was intense. We were in daily, sometimes hourly contact.

In the period afterward, and through the first few years of CCDS, Charlene and I were the staff of the nascent organization.

A Very Good Organizer

Charlene led the organizing work, and then the organization.

Charlene took great pride in being an organizer. And she was very good at it. In fact, extraordinary. Here are a few observations about what made her such a good organizer.

She believed wholeheartedly in the cause. Her actions were not momentary but sustained and fierce and determined. Charlene sought unifying tactics.

Charlene spoke plainly, passionately, from the heart. She was fearless.

Charlene had exceptional charisma. She inspired love and respect not only from the people who agreed with her, but even from some of those with whom she clashed. She inspired people to have confidence in her, and in themselves.

Charlene was generous with her comradeship.

Charlene was constantly learning. Like Walt Whitman, the bard of democracy, Charlene "contained multitudes" – she really heard the stories of diverse people and responded to them.

She never allowed the contradiction and uncertainty of making change to stop her from acting decisively.

What has become of the issues of democracy and socialism?

If you have a big vision, you need a corresponding time scale. We knew that we were living through big events, and that the drama would play out over decades.

Yes, the path is complicated and it's littered with twists and turns, even retreats and defeats and betrayals. And that's okay. It's more than okay. It's righteous. Because ideals of human emancipation must be realized on a global scale and by a profoundly democratic, and therefore messy, process.

Charlene Mitchell Changed My Life

Mael Apollon was a staff member of the Committees of Correspondence for Democracy and Socialism.

By Mael Apollon

I met Charlene Mitchell on the campus of the Borough of Manhattan Community College (BMCC). It was 1993, I was 20 years old and vice-president of the Student Government Association. At the time, we were confronting a continuous assault on the City University of New York's (CUNY) Open Admission Policy. To inform the student body of the threat to Open Admissions, we held numerous public events on the issue; we were doing this as the efforts to limit access to CUNY schools were becoming more apparent, and tuition was getting more expensive and unaffordable for a lot of New York City residents.

One of our Student Government Consultants was Richard Hoyen. Richard had been a staunch advocate for Open Admissions and an activist on the issue since he attended CUNY schools in the 1970s. Richard was also a member of the Committees of Correspondence and spoke highly of Charlene Mitchell. As we pondered over possible panelists who could connect the dots on this economic and racial question, we asked Charlene Mitchell to participate on a panel.

She made the world make sense to us

We held several events for the students on this question, and Charlene Mitchell was always included. Charlene was able to frame what was happening within a larger context. She communicated to students in a manner that the everyday students could understand what was occurring and why. She made things make sense to us. Her ability to do that made students gravitate to her, wanting to converse with her and be around her. I was not immune from this; I, too, wanted to be in her presence.

After meeting her, I was hooked. Charlene Mitchell changed my life. After leaving BMCC, I continued my education, but then I started working in the Committees of Correspondence office part-time and then full-time. I worked there for about seven years, until 2003. Working there expanded my curiosity about the world. Charlene and everyone I worked closely with encouraged me to do what I thought was impossible as a student, like traveling. With their motivation and support, I attended the Fourth World Conference on Women in Beijing, China, and the 14th World Festival of Youth and Students in Cuba. The exposure to these global issues strengthened my comprehension of local matters and helped me in deciding that I wanted to do work that helped improve the lives of others. In 2003, I left CCDS and started working for health care workers' union 1199, and I have been there since.

The passing of Charlene Mitchell is a great loss to us all. She positively impacted the next generation in ways that cannot be measured. But even with her passing on, her legacy lives on within me and others like me. Thank you, Charlene!

Charlene's Realistic Optimism

Robert Greenberg was a staff member of the Committees of Correspondence for Democracy and Socialism.

By Robert Greenberg

One of the most formative periods of my later life was the time I worked at the national office of the CCDS with Charlene. With

Georgia, Mael and for a time, Leslie and Sandra, we had a supportive nest of passionate members, committed to the cause and the organization and, like Charlene, always with care and thoughtfulness for each other. We ran ideas by each other with mutual respect even though we looked up to Charlene with her rich experience as the profound thinker and activist that she was.

What I remember most of that time is Charlene's smile and her gentle voice, her interest in even the smallest detail of our lives, her intense concern that every task be done with attention and care, her most natural way of seeing things in their broader context. What impressed me was her...can I call it realistic optimism? To my memory, Charlene didn't deny the reality of any situation, however bleak, but she wouldn't fail to place it in a context that allowed space for the next steps forward.

At the time the office of the CCDS was at 11 John Street, one block away from the World Trade Center. It was September 11, 2001. Fortunately, none of us had yet arrived at the office that morning. It was Primary Election Day in NYC. I was working for the AFL-CIO supporting voters who were denied the right to vote. Georgia was supporting a candidate. Mael was on her way to the office and got stuck in the subway. Charlene was home.

The office became uninhabitable due to toxic dust. Within a very short period, Charlene's steady hand assured that our work would continue no matter how uncertain everything was. She arranged for us to set up shop at her friend, Lennox Hinds' brownstone in Harlem. Lennox Hinds is an internationally renowned Human rights attorney and a founder of the National Conference of Black Lawyers. Our work continued while New York City recovered. How fortunate we were to share that special time together.Charlene, I will never forget you, and will always treasure the gifts you left all of us.

We Could Count on Charlene

By Bill Fletcher, Jr.

Although I had met Charlene in the early 1990s, we actually worked together in the formation and building of the Black Radical Congress. Charlene was committed to this project and was a strong proponent of unity. Even where there were significant differences, we could count on Charlene to uphold the need for the unity that would keep the project going.

Charlene was a delight to work with, had a marvelous sense of humor, and had a compelling power of analysis.

I was devastated when I heard of her stroke. I felt that we needed her voice and continued presence. Since her stroke I have hoped and prayed for a recovery so that we could have her fully back in the ranks. News of her death struck me like a sharp pin, followed by a deep sadness, recognizing that she would not be returning. Yet it is critical to keep in mind that the world--and the movement--is a better place because of her enormous contributions.

Remembering Charlene Mitchell

By Harry Targ
National Co-Chair, CCDS

I do not like remembrances of people that are more about the writer than the person being celebrated. But in Charlene Mitchell's case, I am going to begin by violating my own criteria to make a point.

Upon arrival at my job at Purdue University in 1967 I became involved in various political activities including working on building a progressive faculty organization, the Anti-War movement, and student rights issues.

In the 1980s, I affiliated with the Committee in Solidarity With the People of El Salvador (CISPES) setting up a local chapter. Also, I participated in the Midwest Scholars Conferences. The major person behind the MSC was Erwin Marquit, Physics Professor and Communist Party member. At a point in time when the Left was "in crisis" because of the collapsing of the Soviet Union in 1990-91, Marquit told me about a new formation, an effort to bring together a multiplicity of sectors of the Left. He said issues of concern to socialists and progressives would be explored at a large meeting that was to be held in Berkeley, California, in 1992.

My wife and I attended that meeting along with hundreds of activists from all sectors of the movement; Communists, peace activists, feminists, anti-racist activists and others, like myself, who were curious about the possibility of building a new left organization. To me that meeting, which led two years later to the founding of the Committees of Correspondence for Democracy and Socialism (CCDS), qualitatively changed my life.

Enter Charlene Mitchell

Now I reflect on the reason for this essay. Among the many activists who organized the program at Berkeley none stood out as much as Charlene Mitchell. She was a presence: strong, passionate, uncompromisingly principled, and dogged in her determination to help lead us to a renewal of a Left in the United States, (and in solidarity with a worldwide left). It was her presence, her energy, her visible strength that convinced me that I had to return home and with others try to build a local CCDS chapter, a statewide network, and to figure out a way to join the national organization. In my mind, being a part of a new socialist organization, one led by an African American woman, was compelling.

Over the years, I began to volunteer for CCDS committees including the National Coordinating Committee (NCC) which met quarterly to decide on organizational policy. Building a new organization out of the post-Soviet 1990s was difficult. It was a time when a multiplicity of issues and programs made organizing complex. CCDS membership included former members of the Communist Party, activists from Trotskyist organizations, and sectors of the peace movement, the feminist movement, anti-racist campaigns and single-issue groups concerned with such topics as banning nuclear weapons and US policy toward Central America. Our NCC meetings were filled with debates about what socialism meant, how we could remain committed to radical goals while continuing our organizational pluralism, what the CCDS relationship to the electoral process should be, and the role of third parties. And Charlene Mitchell, a co-chair and leader of CCDS led the organization through our debates and complicated issues.

Near the end of the 20th century, she initiated a discussion about whether CCDS should identify and commit to a campaign of significance for workers, people of color, and women, a campaign that would help us network with other organizations and campaigns. While virtually every member of the organization was an activist (in fact, the membership collectively represented a history of the left in the United States) she pointed out that CCDS needed a specific program, a campaign to create unity.

The Living Wage Campaign

She proposed CCDS adopt the Living Wage as an issue for us. It was vitally important for workers, Blacks, white, women, young and old as the "prosperity" of the Clinton era did not "trickle down" to the majority of people. And living wage campaigns were sprouting up all around the country. After heated debate, CCDS established a living wage committee. Charlene inspired it, worked on it, recruited members of the committee to gather data, and develop a series of policy recommendations. And the committee set to work encouraging CCDS chapters and individual members to help create living wage committees in their communities.

Also Charlene encouraged debate about where we stood on elections and connecting the "militant minority" of socialists with broader populations of potential progressive activists. The discussion led to a campaign for building a progressive majority. In addition, under her direction, CCDS members, continued to support international solidarity with struggles in Southern Africa, the Caribbean, the Middle East, Central America, Cuba, and the vital transformation of the left in Europe. While many in the leadership of CCDS were part of these campaigns and movements, Charlene Mitchell was clearly the force, the voice behind whatever CCDS achieved.

And for many of us, including new or grassroots activists with no national affiliations, she was the force that mobilized and inspired us.

And she helped us with our local work. She spoke at Purdue University to an event sponsored by the African American Studies program. She keynoted a meeting of socialists at the University of Illinois. She spoke at conferences of progressives in Chicago. Her efforts were tireless. And she worked with others to build the Black Radical Congress.

The impact of her stroke

Charlene occasionally spoke at CCDS meetings of "retiring" or "taking a sabbatical." Most of us put off thinking about the consequences for us. But in 2007, she had a stroke. The impacts on CCDS and the left generally have been incalculable. Of course, CCDS continues and does good work. Mass movements around anti-racism, feminism, a new working class, and for peace have grown in ways none of us could have foreseen at Berkeley.

However, for many of us not having that strong, determined, (sometimes too frank about our failings) leader has been a profound loss. Charlene, an African American woman, a Communist leader, an organizer of the Free Angela Davis campaign, admirer of Paul Robeson, a leader of campaigns to release falsely accused prisoners of a corrupt and racist judicial system, influenced thousands of activists. Despite the fact that she was the Communist Party candidate for president in 1968, she was less visible to the public than many other activists.

But now, reflecting on her history and also what she meant to me, I have to say that Charlene Mitchell was a "giant of the left." And, most importantly, as we reflect on what she meant to most of us, we need to adopt lessons from her work - her passion, her inclusiveness, her organizational determination- as we continue her project.

Remembering Charlene

Leslie Cagan was a staff member of the Committees of Correspondence for Democracy and Socialism

By Leslie Cagan

I had heard about Charlene long before we met or worked together. I knew about the international campaign to free Angela Davis. I knew about the National Alliance Against Racist and Political Repression. I understood that she was a leader in the Communist Party, USA - a proud leader.

I'm a generation younger than Charlene. My politics were shaped by growing up in a leftie, activist family with relatives and close friends that were in the Party, and by coming of age politically in the midst of the cultural explosion and the dynamism of mass movements for freedom and peace in the 1960s. I was part of the New Left and at the same time I wanted to know more about the role the Party had played in the labor movements, economic justice, and anti-racist struggles in earlier decades. Through my involvement in New York City and national coalitions I met some very smart, and very committed, people from the Party. I was never interested in joining the Party, but I listened carefully to what the Party people were saying. I wanted to know more.

One of the people I wanted to know more about, and more from, was Charlene. When I heard about the planning for a national conference to initiate a new socialist organization my ears perked up...this could be interesting. I came out of that weekend gathering as part of the new national leadership team of the Committees of Correspondence for Democracy and Socialism and for the next several years had the opportunity to work closely with Charlene.

We worked closely together in the office of CCDS. She constantly had her eyes on the prize, always thinking strategically about where we needed to focus our energies. At the same time, she never lost sight of the details of the work. Her insightful long-term ideas were always matched with the specifics of what needed to be done today. And she was not hesitant to get her hands dirty, whether that was tackling some major problems or making sure the mailings got sent out on time. (Remember when we used to send mailings out?)

Her moral compass was on the North Star

Most importantly, her moral compass was steadily set on that North Star. She was the living expression of commitment, solidarity, internationalism, working for the greater good and never backing away from a hard fight. Her strategic insights were grounded in the realities of the moment and shaped by a passion for justice and freedom and peace.

I didn't always agree with her, but she usually had smart things to say, things that made me - made us all - think. She held firmly to her ideas and beliefs, so much so that at times it was hard to disagree. I paid attention to what she was saying, the ways she interacted with people, how she ran a meeting, the presentations and speeches I heard her deliver, and more. I was in a Master Class when working with Charlene.

In 2008 my partner, Melanie Kaye/Kantrowitz, and I made a trip to Cuba. Because Melanie had Parkinson's Disease we were able to set up a visit at The International Center of Neurological Restoration (CIREN) with some of the people that are part of their world-renowned program to treat people with PD. While that was quite interesting the highlight of the afternoon came when we were able to have a short visit with Charlene. She had had a serious stroke and was in Havana for treatment. CIREN is set on a sprawling campus that includes housing for people needing intensive treatment for any of a number of medical issues.

Charlene was in the middle of her daily routine of extensive physical therapy so we went to see her in that facility. The minute she saw us that wonderful, welcoming big smile of hers appeared. As important as the years of political work had been, it was the personal connection that meant so much to both Charlene and me. She took a break from the PT and we chatted, even with the difficulty she had speaking. It wasn't a long visit, but I had that special feeling you get when you are with an old friend, a companera.

I learned so much from Charlene and for that I will always be grateful. Charlene was an inspiration for so many of us, and I will always be thankful that I had an opportunity to work so closely with her and to call her my friend.

Charlene Mitchell, Presente!

A Humane Giant

Raymond Suttner served lengthy periods in prison and house arrest for underground and public anti-apartheid activities of the African National Congress, South African Communist Party, and United Democratic Front. He interviewed Charlene Mitchell extensively in 1993. Currently he writes on social and political issues in South Africa.

By Raymond Suttner

A giant is no more. I did not know her so well, but learnt from her conduct and wisdom -a communist in the most humane and humanistic sense of the word.

Tribute to Charlene Mitchell

Daniel Cirera is Senior Researcher in International Relations and Secretary General of the Scientific Council of the Gabriel Péri Foundation, a progressive think tank in France.

By Daniel Cirera
Paris, le 12 février 2023

With Charlene Mitchell we have lost an exceptional woman. Our sadness is immense. I want to share it with those who accompanied her until her last days.

I want to share it with those who, at some point in their commitment, had the chance to benefit from her experience and the firmness of her convictions.
It was a great opportunity for me to speak with Charlene during my stays in New York. It was a privilege to meet the woman who played a leading role in the struggles against racial discrimination, in the defense of Angela Davis and victims of unfair trials. To meet the first African American woman to run for president, who was also nominated by the Communist Party, was not only respectful but also made one reflect on the reality of social and political struggles in the United States.

I remain impressed by the finesse of her questions and her analysis. She wanted to understand how we, in France and in Europe, could best respond to the challenges posed by the upheavals of the world in recent decades. And this with a modesty, a kindness, that I still feel with emotion.

We owe her a tribute for her loyalty to her convictions, her moral and intellectual integrity.

We owe her this tribute for what she brought to our common hopes and struggles. We owe her a tribute for what her life says today to the generations that aspire to a more just society, a society where "the free development of each person is the condition for the free development of all". May her memory contribute to the continuation of her struggles and to sharing them with future generations.